TEXT AT SCALE

CORPUS ANALYSIS IN TECHNICAL COMMUNICATION

T0248365

Foundations and Innovations in Technical and Professional Communication

Series Editor: Lisa Melonçon

Series Associate Editor: Sherena Huntsman

The Foundations and Innovations in Technical and Professional Communication series publishes work that is necessary as a base for the field of technical and professional communication (TPC), addresses areas of central importance within the field, and engages with innovative ideas and approaches to TPC. The series focuses on presenting the intersection of theory and application/practice within TPC and is intended to include both monographs and co-authored works, edited collections, digitally enhanced work, and innovative works that may not fit traditional formats (such as works that are longer than a journal article but shorter than a book).

The WAC Clearinghouse and University Press of Colorado are collaborating so that these books will be widely available through free digital distribution and low-cost print editions. The publishers and the series editors are committed to the principle that knowledge should freely circulate and have embraced the use of technology to support open access to scholarly work.

Other Books in the Series

Han Yu and Jonathan Buehl (Eds.), *Keywords in Technical and Professional Communication* (2023)

Jason C. K. Tham (Ed.), *Keywords in Design Thinking: A Lexical Primer for Technical Communicators & Designers* (2022)

Kate Crane and Kelli Cargile Cook (Eds.), *User Experience as Innovative Academic Practice* (2022)

Joanna Schreiber and Lisa Melonçon (Eds.), *Assembling Critical Components: A Framework for Sustaining Technical and Professional Communication* (2022)

Michael J. Klein (Ed.), *Effective Teaching of Technical Communication: Theory, Practice, and Application* (2021).

TEXT AT SCALE

CORPUS ANALYSIS IN TECHNICAL COMMUNICATION

By Stephen Carradini and Jason Swarts

The WAC Clearinghouse
wac.colostate.edu
Fort Collins, Colorado

University Press of Colorado
upcolorado.com
Denver, Colorado

The WAC Clearinghouse, Fort Collins, Colorado 80523

University Press of Colorado, Denver, Colorado 80203

ISBN 978-1-64215-210-4 (PDF) | 978-1-64215-211-1 (ePub) | 978-1-64642-607-2 (pbk.)

DOI 10.37514/TPC-B.2023.2104

Library of Congress Cataloging-in-Publication Data

Names: Carradini, Stephen, 1988– author. | Swarts, Jason, 1972– author.
Title: Text at scale : corpus analysis in technical communication / Stephen Carradini, Jason Swarts.
Description: Fort Colins, Colorado ; Denver, Colorado : The WAC Clearinghouse ; University Press of Colorado, [2023] | Series: Foundations and innovations in technical and professional communication | Includes bibliographical references.
Identifiers: LCCN 2023042204 (print) | LCCN 2023042205 (ebook) | ISBN 9781646426072 (paperback) | ISBN 9781642152104 (adobe pdf) | ISBN 9781642152111 (epub)
Subjects: LCSH: Communication of technical information—Language. | Corpora (Linguistics) | English language—Discourse analysis.
Classification: LCC T10.5 .C36 2023 (print) | LCC T10.5 (ebook) | DDC 601/.4—dc23/eng/20240302
LC record available at https://lccn.loc.gov/2023042204
LC ebook record available at https://lccn.loc.gov/2023042205

Copyeditor: Don Donahue
Designer: Mike Palmquist
Series Editor: Lisa Melonçon
Series Associate Editor: Sherena Huntsman

The WAC Clearinghouse supports teachers of writing across the disciplines. Hosted by Colorado State University, it brings together scholarly journals and book series as well as resources for teachers who use writing in their courses. This book is available in digital formats for free download at wac.colostate.edu.

Founded in 1965, the University Press of Colorado is a nonprofit cooperative publishing enterprise supported, in part, by Adams State University, Colorado State University, Fort Lewis College, Metropolitan State University of Denver, University of Alaska Fairbanks, University of Colorado, University of Denver, University of Northern Colorado, University of Wyoming, Utah State University, and Western Colorado University. For more information, visit upcolorado.com.

Land Acknowledgment. The Colorado State University Land Acknowledgment can be found at https://landacknowledgment.colostate.edu.

■ Contents

Acknowledgments

Stephen is deeply grateful to Christopher Jones and the members of Writing Studio, Eric Nystrom, David Burel, the IHC Research and Writing Group, Rafael Martinez Orozco, Ian Moulton, and Barbara Carradini. Each went above and beyond the scope of their regular work to aid this manuscript. He would also like to thank Lisa Meloncon, the editorial team at the WAC Clearinghouse, and the reviewers for invaluable help in making this book happen. Finally, many thanks to Jason for being a great mentor and collaborator.

Jason would like to acknowledge the longtime guidance and friendship of his mentor, Cheryl Geisler, who first kindled his interest in methodologies for the systematic study of language and discourse. He would also like to acknowledge the considerable influence of conversations with Dylan Dryer, participants of the Dartmouth Writing Research Seminar, and students in the various sections of ENG 506 (Verbal Data Analysis) he has taught over the years. The ideas in this book would not be nearly as well formed or applied were it not for those interactions. He would also like to thank Lisa Meloncon for her expert input on this manuscript from early idea to finished product, to the reviewers of the manuscript in its various stages, and to Stephen for being an excellent collaborator and an all-around swell guy.

TEXT AT SCALE

CORPUS ANALYSIS IN TECHNICAL COMMUNICATION

1. The Scale of Work in Technical Communication

"Are we there yet?" is a common refrain heard during car trips and discussions about the state of technical communication. Technical communication is no different from fields around the academy that must consistently evaluate their state of the art and state of the practice. Yet the unique contours of technical communication's history and practice make the exercise a fraught one. The establishment of the practice as a part of engineering work, the subsuming of the academic enterprise into English department hierarchies, and the often-complicated relationship between employers and technical communicators collide to make those in the field ponder: do we have things to call our own? Can we delineate what is *ours* and what is *theirs*? Have we clearly articulated the value that this field delivers to the world? Are we a mature field yet? In short: are we there yet?

The answer to "Are we there yet?" is almost necessarily no; the need to ask the question suggests that the asker *knows* we are not there yet, but *cannot believe* that we are not actually there yet. Yet we argue that technical communication is a *maturing* field. By some accounts, the practice of communicating technical knowledge is centuries old (see Durack, 1997; Malone, 2007) but the field of technical communication has been recognized for more than 100 years. This history shows continued advancement in the practice, pedagogy, administration, and research of the activity that we call technical communication. To illustrate, let us give a quick historical sketch of the advancement of technical communication.

Technical communication concerns the delivery of specialized information about and via technology. This activity has been taught and practiced from as long as technology has been created. Aristotle is often mentioned as a forerunner of technical communication, given his systematic informational communication practices. Technical communication began more formally as a trained component of professional engineering in the 1890s (Kynell, 1999). Technology advanced rapidly after the turn of the twentieth century, and technical communication advanced along with it: The Society for Technical Communication notes that "the professional field was firmly established during the First World War, growing out of the need for technology-based documentation in the military, manufacturing, electronic, and aerospace industries" (Society for Technical Communication, n.d.).

The growth of technologies led to a need for teaching technical communication: technical communication pedagogy inside English and communication departments began in the 1950s (Connors, 1982), with the first technical communication program appearing at Rensselaer Polytechnic Institute in 1953 (Melonçon, 2012). Academic journals in technical communication started to appear in the 1980s, while standalone technical communication departments began in the 1990s.

The mass digitization of technical communication in the latter part of the twentieth century greatly increased demand for the skills of technical communicators (even if the job title "technical communicator" has never been prominent). Technical communicators currently fill roles as disparate as grant writer, medical writer, social media specialist, and content strategist (Brumberger & Lauer, 2015), with many technical communicators plying the trade in cutting-edge technology spaces. Programs continue to serve students in their own majors and in other majors, both in in-person and online modes. Thus, the academic enterprise of technical communication has been training professional information delivery specialists for over 130 years, and many industries' desires for those skill sets have grown over that time.

The history of technical communication practice makes a clear case about the advancement of the field. Throughout this advancement, technical communicators have routinely taken stock of technical communication practice and pedagogy, assessing what the field needs to do to mature into its own freestanding, fully developed concern. Often, factors have been found to be lacking, such as a lack of established practices, a lack of professional certification/gatekeeping, or a central topic of the field. The various concerns shift over time, as the field moves to address the previous concerns.

Where advancement of technical communication practice resulted in the development of a range of practices and an overall expansion of the field to meet a variety of ends, questions of maturation have turned our attention inward, leading to conversations about best practices, professional certification, central topics, and core methodologies. These are questions rooted in disciplinary identity, which will surprise no one who follows such conversations. It will also surprise no one that these questions are still difficult to answer after all of these years. The growing professional record of technical communication practice promises that these questions will never become easier to answer. Yet we are at a spot where some cornerstones have been established and new progress can be made.

Technical communication has certainly reached a point where we have engaged in enough professional and teaching practice that we are no longer figuring out the principles of what works. We have done enough now that it is profitable for us to look back on all that has been accomplished to see what we have learned and, from that, to project a path forward. This inward look is a move that results in better self-awareness, moving technical communication from being more of an inductive field (focused on doing, trial and error, and invention) to being equal parts inductive and deductive (reflecting, learning from successes and failures, theorizing, and framing future practices).

This motion toward field maturation is already present and we are certainly not the first to point it out. Our niche is to suggest an approach that enables critical reflection on what the field has accomplished without oversimplifying the scope of the field. The need we identify in this chapter and respond to throughout this book is one of adopting methods of scale that are capable of accounting for the scale and diversity of our field's practices. We will show how corpus analysis' technical capabilities and techniques can help address research questions about the field at large and individual research areas.

To establish the value of a corpus analytic methodology for field maturation, we first need to sketch a picture of the challenge posed by the scale of technical communication practice. It is scale that makes it difficult to obtain an overview of the field and observe the many currents that comprise it. The development of technical communication into a large-scale enterprise began more than fifty years ago: As society digitized in the 1970s, technical communication began a multi-decade shift from predominantly print products toward a mix of print and digital products (Carradini, 2022). The practices that produce digital technical communication products have been advancing and maturing over the last 50 years. One outcome of this shift to digital is a new ability to create and store of massive amounts of texts. The primary work of technical communication is now created, iterated, and delivered online. Online work encourages the proliferation of texts because the production and delivery constraints of online content are far fewer than the constraints of print content. Old genres have gone online, and in many cases they have stayed available online for extremely long amounts of time.

In addition to moving old genres online, technical communicators have created new genres in emerging online spaces. The genre of the forum post has become an integral part of technical communication work, as users relay technical concerns to organizations in idiosyncratic ways (Swarts, 2018). The crowdfunding proposal is a new genre that transforms the social and technical aspects of grant writing to a great extent: proposals on websites like Kickstarter and IndieGoGo allow writers to make an appeal to a public audience of potential funders (Carradini & Fleischmann, 2023). Podcasts and their attendant transcripts offer new ways to deliver oral and written information. These new genres reflect significant areas of development in technical communication practice and research, which add to the proliferation of texts.

Finally, the standard workplace communication practices of technical communication are now digital. Text is created as a byproduct of standard communicative interactions of organizations when essential operations move online, and much of that (such as email or Slack chat threads) is stored indefinitely. Thus, the number of texts in technical communication has proliferated rapidly as online practice has developed. The now-commonplace nature of online activity that gave rise to this amount of text suggests that the proliferation is likely to continue.

Given these three drivers of text proliferation in technical communication organizations (old genres going online, new genres developing, standard digital communications being stored), many organizations involved in technical communication have amassed huge amounts of digital and digitized texts. Some companies have produced decades of digital work stored in online content management systems. These CMSs can include huge numbers of policies, reports, product-related content, social media posts, user comments, interview notes, and video transcripts fill practitioners' content management systems.

Technical communicators don't just write copious amounts of texts, however. They also do things with those texts. Doing things with texts, and especially managing texts, requires a reflective understanding of what texts do, how they are used, and what values and motives they represent. Yet management, categorization, delivery, and storage are not the only practices affected (Hackos, 2002; Halvorson & Rach, 2012). Technical communicators must consider how to communicate with customers, attract funding, shape user experience, communicate identity, and share knowledge amid the troves of content held by their organizations.

Academic technical communicators also have varied needs within this deluge of texts. Digital and digitized research articles, conference presentations, syllabi, web content, student papers, and class materials have accumulated over more than half a century in academic technical communication. An ever-growing amount of academic research identifies opportunities to further aid practitioners, engages with underrepresented topics and voices, develops research practices, and considers new ethical concerns. Researchers must consult this consistently growing body of literature to understand the state of research topics and develop further projects. Beyond research, teachers and administrators assess the vast amount of text that classes collectively create to evaluate students and appraise how well teaching practices prepare students for an ever-changing workplace. With the amount of text in each of these categories growing every day, academic technical communicators need methods and tools to help make sense of this ocean of texts.

Ultimately, we argue in this book that corpus analysis is a method that can help technical communicators of all types respond productively to the immense amount of text created by the various arms of the field of technical communication. This method can aid in reflective study of technical communication to help further develop our maturing professional practice and academic field.

Corpus analysis offers a way to approach the work of technical communication at the source material's level of scale by allowing analysis of more texts than an individual or team could read alone. Researchers can then draw out insights that hold across large numbers of texts and apply those insights to the concerns at hand. In this book, we explain concepts, describe techniques, give examples, and outline potential applications of corpus analysis for technical communication practice, research, teaching, and administration. We offer emerging technical communication scholars, established faculty, and practitioners a way to further develop and maintain awareness of their work at scale.

■ A Brief Sketch of Corpus Analysis

As a brief introduction, the method of corpus analysis helps researchers study collections of texts larger than an individual could analyze alone. A corpus (singular) or corpora (plural) must be organized around unifying characteristics (such as topic, professional organization, chronological window, or all of these together) and converted to machine-readable text. Researchers use various analytic techniques to quantitatively identify patterns of words, phrases, and other discourse objects from a corpus that can support analysis of their use patterns.

For example, a researcher could analyze a corpus of 50,000 comments from a user help forum on a piece of software. To build the corpus, the researcher could download all the comments from the content management system and convert them to .txt files. To conduct analysis, the next step would be to upload the corpus to an analysis tool such as Lancsbox or AntConc, then generate analyses of word frequency in the corpus (the baseline first step of many corpus analysis efforts). After the initial step of word frequency, scholars can conduct analyses that build on those results. One analysis could identify words that appear with unexpected frequency in the corpus (as compared to a different corpus for reference), words that are unexpectedly absent in relation to the reference corpus, and words that commonly appear together. Further investigation with these analysis methods can help the researcher discover in those forum comments topics that users frequently need help with, errors or challenges they often experience, or issues that are changing in frequency over time. These insights can help identify areas of documentation needs that could be too cumbersome to do through manual inspection of the forum comments or too prone to bias depending on how individual users might be queried for the same information.

Thus, corpus analysis allows the field to identify and find evidence of its practices in text while also allowing assessment of those practices at a scale that allows us to reflect on what we know and what we do. Much corpus analysis has already been conducted in technical communication (Boettger & Ishizaki, 2018; Orr, 2006). Scholars have investigated how specialized terminology regarding search engine optimization is translated into Spanish (Laursen et al., 2014); what rhetorical strategies are included in writing templates for professional letters (Kaufer & Ishizaki, 2006); "how corpora can help copy editors adopt a rhetorical view of prescriptive usage rules" (Smith, 2022, p. 194); how passive style is used in civil engineering practitioner documents, with the goal of teaching writing more effectively (Conrad, 2017); and more over the past 30 years. Even though technical communication is not new to corpus analysis, we argue that the practitioner and scholarly concerns that come with the maturation of the field call for more corpus analysis.

Although technical communication has an established body of corpus analysis work, even more corpus analysis has been conducted outside technical communication, in writing studies more broadly. The comparison to writing studies more generally is important because researchers in that field have already reached the same point of historical development and maturation as technical communication, and they have already been using reflective corpus analysis to theorize, to establish best practices, to guide future experience. We draw on these and other studies to demonstrate the capabilities of corpus analysis and suggest how they could be turned toward technical communication's goals and ends.

The first step in the research method is to pick a technique of quantitative analysis. Frequency is a common first place. Identifying the most frequent words in a corpus has many applications for research. Some research questions can be answered through frequency alone, such as: "what are the most common adjectives and adverbs in a set of user help tickets?" This information can help identify areas of text that indicate users' emotional experiences regarding a software. Frequency allows us to answer some of the more basic reflective questions: what do we write about and how often?

Another technique is keyness, which uses statistical analysis of the frequency of terms in two corpora to determine words that are more "key" to one corpus than the other. This technique can be used to answer questions such as "What words and phrases differ between two sets of reports published ten years apart on climate change mitigation?" This information could show change or lack thereof in an organization's attempts to help mitigate the effects of climate change. Here too, keyness allows a kind of reflection. In addition to revealing what the field writes about, keyness tells us what our body of work is about, what is important, and what differentiates the field from other fields.

A third technique is collocation analysis, which shows researchers what words often occur near each other. This technique can help answer questions such as "what nouns or pronouns appear nearby conditional words (if, might, could, would) in our content management system," where this information could be used to assess accessible language in healthcare documents.

These three techniques each point toward words, phrases and other discourse objects that can be relevant to answer research questions or repay further quantitative or qualitative study (Archer, 2009a). As with frequency and keyness, collocation facilitates reflection by elucidating how keywords combine into larger conceptual units. It allows us to name what complex topics have preoccupied us as practitioners and academics. These techniques reveal emergent patterns in texts that represent the outcomes of our professional and academic practices. These patterns are a form of evidence that supports reflective analysis of what those practices are and perhaps how they have changed over time. We will discuss these techniques and their application in Chapters 2, 3, and 5.

The Possibilities of Corpus Analysis in Technical Communication

In the sections that follow, we show how corpus analysis can be specifically valuable for practitioners, researchers, teachers, and administrators of technical communication. Corpus analysis can assist researchers of technical communication in conducting research on existing topics and emerging topics. Teachers and administrators of technical communication can use corpus analysis to assess and enhance teaching and programmatic outcomes in a variety of ways. Corpus analysis can also affect many different types and areas of work for the practitioner, such as in handling user feedback, tackling content management, and conducting large-scale technical editing tasks. Gaining reflective insight about our practices can help us be more deliberate and intentional in those practices as well as critical of those practices, as warranted.

To be clear, the specific topics that follow are illustrations of corpus analytic techniques that can allow practitioners and scholars alike to reflect on what the field has accomplished, what those accomplishments may mean, and project from them to additional questions. It is not our aim to set an agenda for field research; given the many strands of technical communication research, many agendas should be set. We will argue in the final chapter that agenda setting may be a necessary future step, considering the effort required to build and maintain corpora. For now, we hope to point toward areas where corpus analysis could productively aid ongoing research efforts, acknowledging and expecting that each area's researchers will find more ways forward for each topic.

▊ Research

Corpus analysis can be used on corpora of texts representing professional activity. Technical communication researchers can use corpus analysis' techniques of identification and re-contextualization to reflect on what we have learned through and across research studies. To begin, we will discuss existing and emerging areas of interest for technical communication.

▊ Existing Area of Interest: Genre

Corpus analysis can extend and support work in well-established areas of technical communication research. Topics such as genre and medical communication are two of many areas that could have open questions further analyzed by large-scale, document-based research.

Technical communication scholars have been interested in genres of technical communication for 40+ years. And genre questions tend to be big questions, the answers to which are intended to give us insight into entire genre types, genre systems, and historical eras of genre development. Genre gains power as an explanatory concept when conventions can be displayed as common across many instances. S. Scott Graham, et al. (2015) note of a big-data approach to genre that uses statistics: "Characteristics that may be invisible at the level of a single text may become visible in a statistical representation that takes into account an enormous number of texts" (p. 92) This statement is true of corpus analysis as well. Because corpus analysis can reveal generic conventions at scale and show in detail the elements of a trend that are present across a large number of documents, the results contribute to our ability to explicitly discuss what is customary or routine. By the same reasoning, corpus analysis can help falsify genre claims by revealing patterns that may seem interesting but are isolated and idiosyncratic: "Genres can be defined . . . with more precision (i.e., which features are actually typical across the genre, not just in the particular text one may have analyzed?)" (Graham et al., 2015, p. 92). Thus, corpus analysis can help confirm, support, and extend the findings of qualitative genre research by investigating large corpora of genred text.

Corpus analysis also offers ways to reflect, deliberately, on what we know as a field and our own genres (e.g., consider Dryer, 2019); in this specific case, it allows researchers to develop and extend genre research by considering these open questions with more examples across an ever-widening range of genres.

Genre scholars already conduct comparisons across methods (Campbell et al., 2020; Miller et al., 2018;) or on larger data sets (Robles, 2018) as ways of confirming findings, but many open questions in genre can benefit from large-scale analysis. Genre scholars are interested in understanding how new genres work, particularly new genres on the internet (Mehlenbacher, 2019; Robles, 2018); how genre operates in multilingual and multinational settings (Hodges & Seawright, 2019); how emotions interact with genres (Miller et al., 2018; Weedon, 2020); and the evergreen concern of how to teach genres (Kim & Olson, 2020; Tardy et al., 2020).

Each of these expansions in the study of genre builds on existing research. As that body of research grows, our capacity to gain an overview of those genre practices, and to examine large scale patterns and changes over time, grows. So too does the challenge of engaging in such investigations grow. Corpus analysis can be used for meta-research: research on the research. Meta-research makes connections across large bodies of research to assess trends or patterns in the research. Technical communication scholars can use corpus analysis to reflect on what we cover in our research and how we have covered it. This reflective practice can help identify points where we can steer the field's research in new directions.

Technical communication scholars can and do use corpus analysis and related types of large data analysis for meta-research. Researchers frequently mine corpora of technical communication research to identify disciplinary issues. Ryan K. Boettger and Erin Friess (2016) investigated "the content alignment (or lack thereof) among academics and practitioners" as exemplified in work published in academic and practitioner outlets. They found little content alignment via their quantitative content analysis of 1,048 articles, suggesting that the field is fragmented in its research interests. This comparative analysis once again demonstrates the value of contrasting corpora as a technique.

Kate White et al. (2015) conducted a quantitative content analysis of nine textbooks and 1,073 articles from five technical communication journals using keyword searches to identify "the treatment of gender and feminism in technical, business, and workplace writing studies" (p. 27; also, the title of the article). After reviewing content associated with the terms "female, feminist, gender, gendered, cross-gender, gender-neutral, sex/sexes, sexual, sexism, sexist, and woman/women" (p. 34), the authors argue that "the discourse seems to paint a false picture of the workplace as neutral and nongendered" (p. 49). This article used a quantitative approach (checking books and articles for the existence of terms) to drive a qualitative analysis of what the limited number of book sections and articles about gendered issues meant for the field. This combination of quantitative and qualitative approaches is a productive one that we will discuss further in Chapter 2.

In another meta-study, Heather Noel Turner (2022) conducted a corpus analysis to compare the topics of the ATTW conference presentations against topics found in the *Technical Communication Quarterly* journal, finding ways that the journal topics and conference topics support and diverge from each other. This type of comparative corpus analysis allows for clear differentiation between corpora. Turner used keyness as a way to determine degrees of difference in terminology use between the ATTW corpus and the TCQ corpus. Building on Turner's work, conference content could be further mined. The text of technical communication books (building on the work of Rude, 2009) and textbook content (following White et al., 2015) are two more of the unintentional repositories of data waiting to be activated as a corpus and to deliver field-level insights.

Corpus-based meta-research can also be conducted to build theories, as Julie A. Corrigan and David Slomp (2021) do. They conducted a "critical review of writing scholarship from the past 50 years" to "synthesize the significant scholarship in the field in order to advance theory" (p. 143). Their content analysis of "109 texts revealed that the following writing knowledge domains have predominated the literature: metacognitive, critical discourse, discourse, rhetorical aim, genre, communication task process, and substantive knowledge" (p. 143), which they used to build a new theory about "the knowledge domains that constitute expertise in writing" in a digital age (p. 167). Technical communication scholars can also use corpus analysis for theory-building meta-research by identifying terms or phrases from a corpus of literature to examine further. Areas such as social media, user experience, and other areas with many contributing theories from varied fields could benefit from this type of journal article meta-analysis. Integrative literature reviews, which painstakingly synthesize journal articles on topics (Andersen & Batova, 2015a; Lauren & Schreiber, 2018) could benefit from the identification aspects of corpus analysis.

Another area where corpus analysis can be effective is medical communication, which has been a part of technical communication since before 2000 (Connor, 1993). Research on medical communication demonstrates that corpus analysis can be used on transcripts of oral communication as well as written documents. For example, Ellen Barton (2004) studied the oral communication of oncologists by drawing on transcripts of 12 "front stage" conversations inside clinical rooms and 33 "backstage" conversations between medical professionals and the researcher. Barton found that "the oral genre of treatment discussion in oncology encounters is organized to allow practitioners to do, appear to do, or avoid doing difficult work like presenting a prognosis" (p. 67). Barton discovered this finding by analyzing the structure of the oral presentations that oncologists gave to patients and family, as well as comparing the content of the message to the patients with the content of the messages spoken outside the clinic room to other professionals and the researcher. This comparative method allowed Barton to develop a critical awareness of differences between the two, in order to ask why those differences might be important.

Corpus analysis also allows cross-referencing of large amounts of texts against other data. For example, Graham et al. (2015) conducted "statistical genre analysis" on a large corpus of transcripts and metadata from Federal Drug Administration drug advisory committee meetings. They found that "the use of efficacy data seems to lower the chance of approval, whereas a greater presence of conflict of interest increases the probability of approval" (p. 89), which "indicate[s] the need for changes to FDA conflict-of-interest policies" (p. 70). The ability to cross-reference the content of texts with metadata (in this case, metadata being the outcome of voting on the approval of a drug as a result of the meeting) led to an insight on how the content of the meetings may have affected the outcome of voting. Researchers can conduct this type of cross-referencing outside medical documentation for proposed policy documents concerning issues of technical communication interest that may have a range of outcomes (passed, tabled, returned to committee, rejected), as well as emerging proposal genres such as crowdfunding campaigns (Ishizaki, 2016) that have largely binary outcomes.

Emerging Areas of Interest: Social Justice

A reflection on what a maturing field has done can also present the opportunity to recognize what has been unaddressed and what has yet to be done. Reflection can be agenda-setting. One example of this outcome for reflection is the growing focus on social justice over the last 20 years. The term "social justice" did not appear in the abstracts of five technical communication journals from the period 2000–2005, but appeared in journal abstracts thereafter (Carradini, 2022). Social justice work in technical communication seeks to be productively critical of and to intervene in the ways that writing, discourse, and actions based on discourses can systematically exclude or marginalize particular readers and reader experiences.

Research methods that call us to reconsider "established" knowledge, make textual problems visible, catalog the scope of problems, and illumine starting points for interventions can be an aid to social justice research. Corpus analysis is one such research method (among others). Thus, corpus analysis can fit in with the work that scholars of social justice do and are calling for.

First, the conceptual basis of corpus analysis can aid the overall goals of social justice work. In Emily January Petersen and Rebecca Walton's 2018 call for critical, feminist analysis in addition to critical action we identify a space for corpus analysis: "We agree that action is needed to redress inequities, but we also see a potential danger in the field's shift toward critical action if that shift is not carefully informed by critical analysis" (p. 418). To that end, corpus analysis can be used in critical ways to support and encourage critical action. Researchers can produce studies that identify issues in texts that need addressing, review field-level practices to make sure social justice practices are achieving their desired outcomes (Itchuaqiyaq & Matheson, 2021), and make connections between topics in corpora that appear comparatively infrequently and actions that could be taken to redress those textual practices. In short, corpus analysis can illumine potential ways forward for social justice efforts through critical reflection on large amounts of texts.

Corpus analysis also calls us to reconsider "established" knowledge through critical reflection through all parts of the research. The process of thinking through a corpus analytic study creates moments for critical reflection before the data is even collected. Considering what constitutes a representative corpus of content for study (see Chapter 4) requires researchers to have an educated sense of how to build a corpus that represents both the range and diversity of the field and its practices. Daniela Agostinho et al. (2019) remind us that any large collection of data is a form of archive, and all archives can have serious limitations and exclusions. Historically, archives have "overlooked the experiences of women and queers" while archives related to slavery and colonialism expose "both the capture and exclusion of people of colour in and from archives and the kind of knowledge that can be gleaned from the archives of the ruling classes, archives that dehumanise those under colonial rule" (p. 424). While data gathered without careful attention to what is going into the corpus can reproduce these sorts of inequities, gathering data that effectively represents the range of content in a situation can produce corpora that help lead to research that helps identify and, ideally, correct injustices of this type.

This type of pre-collection reflection is necessary because concerns of bias in corpus analysis are legitimate: if bias goes into the data, then bias can come out in the findings (O'Neil, , 2016). This concern features prominently when professionals use "big data" for controversial ends, such as training artificial intelligence to skim pools of job applicants' resumes (Miller, 2019), analyzing loan applications (Lane, 2017), handing down sentencing suggestions in courts (Tashea, 2017), and ever-more invasive iterations on this theme (Stephens, 2018). Whatever biases exist in training data will be reproduced in the results the algorithm produces. Constructing corpora carefully (Chapter 4) and conducting work that identifies bias can work against these trends.

Next, corpus analysis can help make social justice concerns visible in large amounts of texts. Work identifying systemic bias and discrimination, systemic racism, systemic misogyny, systemic homophobia, systemic classism, systemic ableism, and more can build on qualitative work, extending and supporting these concerns to develop a wider picture of the problem. This kind of language is said and printed in public and private spaces, which perpetuates casual discrimination and bias of all sorts. This sort of language can persist unless we first make an effort to locate it, which could be accomplished by investigating the possibility of overrepresentation bias via an analysis of keywords. Underrepresentation bias could also be sought through an analytic method called "negative keywords," or evaluating a corpus of text against a prepared corpus that reflects an expected dispersion of a term or phrase tested against a study corpus for comparative over/under representation. Understanding the trends of bias, overrepresentation, and underrepresentation in texts can support claims that certain types of text include bias against certain types of people in specific ways. From there, interventions can be designed on the local or individual scale to address the issue.

Beyond aiding researchers in identifying certain types of problems in text, corpus analysis can help researchers catalog the scope of problems by quantitatively displaying the scale of those types of problems. Qualitative analysis can identify findings in a small-to-medium amount of data, and corpus analytic techniques can help researchers test to identify if those practices are present in large amounts of data. Corpus analysis is very well suited to establishing mathematical relationships between words, such as identifying if one word is much more frequent than another or if one word is unusually absent in a corpus (in relation to a reference corpus). These tracking and confirmation efforts can help establish the scope of a problem or interest area over a large set of data. This results in research that can determine if those relationships appear across a large amount of data or are idiosyncratic to a specific text, condition, or situation.

This type of work already exists: Godwin Y. Agboka (2021) used a quantitative content analysis to point out the scope of the problem of using the word "subject" to describe the human participants of technical communication research. Likewise, Barton et al. (2018) used content analysis to identify the circumscribed ways that community members contributed to research ethics discussions concerning their neighborhood. While these analyses were not corpus analytic, they were large-scale approaches to text analysis that can reveal patterns of activity in text (e.g., portrayal and participation) that point toward topics of interest, findings, and suggestions for action.

Corpus analysis findings can also help illumine starting points for interventions in social justice concerns. After analyzing 450,000 online comments from *New York Times* articles, for example, John R. Gallagher et al. (2020) point out social justice interventions that could take place in the space of online content moderation. While the authors acknowledge the complexities and difficulties of localizing their ideas to individual websites (pp. 167–168), their findings present a starting point for more local interventions to develop and grow in relation to this concern. The authors do not explicitly use corpus analysis as a method, but they do demonstrate the value of a large-scale analysis of text (similar to corpus approaches).

These steps of reconsidering "established" knowledge, making social justice concerns visible in texts, cataloging the scope of the problem, and illumining starting points for local interventions are each demonstrated by Cana Uluak Itchuaqiyaq and Breeanne Matheson (2021). The authors began by reconsidering "established" knowledge, as they "used corpus analysis techniques to investigate the field's working definition of 'decolonial' as it relates to methods and methodologies" (p. 21). The reason to reconsider this "established" knowledge, they argue, is that "TPC scholarship designed using decolonial frameworks lacks a clear, centralized definition and may overgeneralize and/or marginalize Indigenous concerns" (p. 20).

Itchuaqiyaq and Matheson (2021) employed corpus analysis to make visible a concern they had about texts: "we already suspected that many of the texts would use decolonial as a euphemism for social justice or humanitarian work because of our previous exposure to this particular critique coming from scholars Tuck and Yang (2012)" (p. 21). Their corpus analysis cataloged the scope of the problem, identifying that this concept did hold across a range of texts (p. 24). This finding prompted the authors to suggest starting points for local interventions, as they "propose a centralized definition of 'decolonial' that focuses on rematriation of Indigenous land and knowledges" (p. 20). Thus, the process of corpus analysis in this article moved from a reconsideration of knowledge via an initial concern about a concept, through making the concept visible via analytic techniques and a subsequent confirmation of the concept in a variety of texts, to suggestions on how to redress the issues raised as a result of the analysis. This exemplar shows that corpus analytic work can help social justice researchers be productively critical of and intervene in the ways that writing, discourse, and actions based on discourses can systematically exclude or marginalize particular readers and reader experiences.

Emerging Areas of Interest: User Experience

Corpus analysis can aid other areas of technical communication practice as well, such as user experience (UX). User experience currently has little published corpus analysis work conducted about it. Yet the nature of UX suggests that researchers may use forms of large-scale analysis (such as content analysis) to work with the texts representing many user experience tests. Assessing many tests at once could reveal holistic insights about users. User experience research takes many forms, with some of the more prominent being researcher-guided speak-aloud protocols tests. Technical communicators often record these complex tests for analysis purposes. If the test is of a computer-based item, then the user's screen, the user's voice, and the researcher's voice may be recorded separately or together. The oral recordings can be transcribed (automatically by a machine or by a human) and used as the basis of corpus analysis. Florentina Armaselu (2022) analyzed a corpus of recorded user experience tests regarding a software for viewing historical documents, identifying four different categories of users as a result of their transcribed oral responses to the software. This type of analysis can be implemented in a wide variety of user experience test transcriptions, regardless of the number of tests.

Corpus size may be small in user experience research, as user experience tests for a specific piece of software or website often include fewer than 100 tests (although the number can range into the hundreds or thousands). However, corpus analysis of the transcripts of many studies (which could range into the hundreds or thousands) may be able to tell a researcher about the guidance habits of researchers in think-aloud protocols. Alternatively, a corpus of usability test transcripts regarding many versions of a software could be structured chronologically to investigate how users' difficulties or successes in the software changed over time. Similarly, a chronological corpus of that type could be investigated for changing habits of researchers' guidance over time. Chronological analyses can develop over time to become more meaningful as the researcher collects more data, because in many cases a long chronological window can demonstrate a phenomena's persistence, growth, or decline more meaningfully than a small window.

User experience research can also be conducted in other ways. Phillip Brooker et al. (2016) use corpus analysis to identify "user experiences of epinephrine auto-injectors ('epipens')" from a small corpus of posts on Twitter (around 4,000 tweets over 68 days) (p. 8). They argue that the corpus approach:

> allowed us to explore a broad topic of interest—epipens—without relying on simple term frequency to point us in any particular direction. Navigating around the cluster map in this way, analysts can sift their data for "needles in haystacks"—here, this provided insight into user experiences with epipens unlikely to be uncovered with more formal search terms (i.e., "weight" and "size"). (p. 9)

Thus, user experience information can be gleaned from social media sites, help forums, website-hosted email forms, and other areas of user-generated content via corpus analysis.

Corpus analysis may also help provide perspective on emerging trends in professional technical communication. For example, entrepreneurship is another topic of interest associated with volumes of text. One type of analysis of entrepreneurship has focused on the genres of entrepreneurial activity (Spartz & Weber, 2015; Spinuzzi et al., 2014). As with the study of genres mentioned above, corpus analysis could reveal aspects of entrepreneurial communication and activity across a wide set of examples. Identifying distinctive aspects of successful or unsuccessful entrepreneurial activities or communication habits could be instructive for entrepreneurs and for those seeking to teach entrepreneurs.

Transcripts of meetings between entrepreneurs and funders that take place after funding cycles could help researchers identify ways that entrepreneurs signal success or make efforts to repair relationships amid difficulties. From a pedagogical perspective, instructions on how to be entrepreneurial abound; using a corpus analysis to research what consistent claims, ideas, or patterns are present across many different forms of pedagogy (popular books, textbooks, websites, transcribed online videos, etc.) could develop categories or meta-categories

(categories of categories) for the types of concerns that successful or unsuccessful entrepreneurs have. This point about meta-research leads us to the next category of research where corpus analysis can be particularly valuable.

Education

Academic technical communication includes research, pedagogy, and administration. Corpus analysis can help technical communicators reflect on our accumulated pedagogical and administrative practices. Many technical communication programs have been active for long enough that we can use the accumulation of texts over time to assess the efficacy of our teaching practices. In fact, many studies of first-year writing in the composition sub-field of writing analytics and its attendant *Journal of Writing Analytics* have already shown that corpus analysis can productively aid the teaching of student writing (e.g., Aull, 2017; Holcomb & Buell, 2018). Administration of pedagogy can also be aided by corpus analysis, as the texts students produce (Peele, 2018), syllabi, or other artifacts of teaching can be analyzed to help programs best fulfill their remit to educate emerging technical communication students.

Pedagogy

Teachers can use corpus analysis on large amounts of text to aid student development in a variety of ways. Lexical elements of student writing can be made meaningful on their own or in comparison to the corpora of work of more advanced writers. Teaching individual argumentative strategies, citation moves, or practical elements of various genres scratch the surface of the possible findings (and attendant teaching outcomes) that corpus analysis can contribute to pedagogy.

Decades of pedagogical development and implementation in technical communication has produced a potentially immense amount of data on student progress and student development. Technical communication teachers can consult this data to understand what our pedagogy has focused on and how students have used the skills they have been taught. This work requires corpora, and technical communication scholars have begun to collect, curate, and investigate student work at scale to create corpora. Ryan K. Boettger and Stephanie Wulff created a corpus of technical communication student writing that allows investigation of how students respond to prompts, use language, invoke topics, and more (Boettger & Wulff, 2022). Similarly, Bradley Dilger, Michelle McMullin, and others have developed CROW (Corpus & Repository of Writing) to "create a web-based archive for research and professional development in applied linguistics and rhetoric & composition" (Staples et al., 2021), while USF Writes includes a large corpus of student technical and professional writing that the Department of English at the University of South Florida uses for "continual assessment processes, and programmatic and pedagogical improvement" (University of South Florida, 2023). Researchers initially developed the Stanford Study of Writing

(SSW) corpus for qualitative analysis, but Noah Arthurs (2018) used quantitative analysis to investigate a subset of the corpus. The author found that corpus analytic techniques revealed stances students took toward their topics, the topics of their writing, and elements of sentence complexity. Given these features and metadata associated with the texts about the students' characteristics, the study "characterize[d] the development of the SSW participants across four years of undergraduate study, specifically gaining insight into the different trajectories of humanities, social science, and STEM students" (p. 138). These findings provide insight into the process of writing development and can be useful for curricular development and course design.

Analysis of student work outside established corpora can also directly help develop pedagogical outcomes. Individual instructors can conduct analysis of students' papers over an individual assignment, class section, or semester's worth of classes to evaluate elements of writing practice. (These are sometimes called ad-hoc corpora in relation to permanent corpora, but ad-hoc corpora seem to be more common than permanent corpora, due to the complexity of corpus creation in large-scale, permanent corpora; see Anne Lise Laursen et al. [2014].) Some grammar elements of writing, such as nominalizations and conjunction use, are readily identifiable and can be assessed in relation to desired pedagogical outcomes. More complex analysis is possible as well, focusing on words frequently appearing together or words frequently appearing in the beginning of the assignment that may allow the instructor to understand how students are taking up the class information into their own writing processes.

Barton (1993) demonstrated how analysis of an ad-hoc corpora of student argumentation from a university writing proficiency requirement could help identify differences between the approaches of writers who vary in experience. Comparing student writing with that of writers writing in the *Chronicle of Higher Education*, Barton (1993) focused on the writers' use of evidentials: "words and phrases that express attitudes toward knowledge," such as *must*, *should*, and *I believe that* (p. 745). Through a discourse analysis comparing 100 student papers to 100 *Chronicle* opinion articles, Barton demonstrates that experienced academic writers "adopt an epistemological stance that privileges knowledge defined as a product of contrast" (p.754) (as demonstrated by use of phrases like *as a result* and *undeniable*) while student writers "more consistently assume an epistemological stance that privileges knowledge defined as a product of shared social agreement" (p.765) (as demonstrated by use of phrases like *today in America* or *most will agree that*). While this finding demonstrates an area where young writers can be taught conventions of academic discourse, Barton identifies an opportunity for pedagogical reflection, suggesting that "we may wish to ask ourselves why we seem to be rewarding our student writers primarily for reproducing our own contrastive and competitive epistemological stance" (p. 766). Barton's study is successful because it relies on analysis of two contrasting corpora to identify, classify, and illustrate (with examples) instances of evidentials. These findings can relate directly to pedagogical efforts by individual teachers in technical communication classrooms. Other similar studies could produce findings concerning writing in technical communication: instruction sets, regulatory writing, grant writing, social media writing, and more.

A similar example concerns how corpus analysis can support pedagogical choices related to genre knowledge and genre writing skill in first-year writing. Laura Aull (2017) compared two different types of student writing: argumentative vs explanatory. Aull identified "generalized, interpersonal, and persuasive discourse in argumentative essays versus more specified, informational, and elaborated discourse in explanatory writing, regardless of course or task" (p.2). This type of finding relates both to genre analysis and pedagogy, as work of this type can be used to identify specific types of arguments or moves in genres to teach them to students.

Along the same lines, Steven Walczak (2017) developed tools to distinguish between the prose of different types of genres, creating exercises for students to be able to develop information literacy by distinguishing text from different genres (newspapers, magazines, and journal articles). Walczak's work demonstrates how student use of corpus analysis can directly relate to genre learning.

Also adopting a pedagogical focus, Ian G. Anson et al. (2019) used corpus analytic tools and custom-built tools to study text recycling in published academic research: a researcher's use of their own previously published sections of text in new academic work. Their custom tools allowed them to identify close matches or subtle changes in sentences (instead of exact copying) that would reflect different types of text recycling for different purposes. Understanding the purposes and contexts of text recycling could help student writers recognize conventions of different discourse communities in regards to the practice of text recycling.

Similarly, Ryan Omizo and William Hart-Davidson (2016a) created tools to identify the "hedginess" of published academic research writing, identifying one goal of the work as: "For learners, tools like the Hedge-O-Matic might make explicit the kinds of patterns that are expected by scientific discourse communities" (n. p.).

Corpus analysis has also been used to suggest effective types of mentorship for advanced students. Omizo and Hart-Davidson (2016b) "explore[d] the possibilities of using computational methods to create an assistive environment for advisor-advisee mentoring in academic writing" (p. 487). They identified "lexical patterns and rhetorical uses of the in-text citations" to create categories of citation moves (Extraction, Grouping, and Author[s] as Actant[s]), then compared these moves between three dyads of advisor-advisee writing. They sought "to automate the discovery of a generic baseline for citational moves among academic mentoring relationships" (p. 507). Corpus analysis can replicate this process to determine the progress of advanced technical communication students. This process can also compare students' failed grant campaigns to successful ones for evidence of stylistic differences that may have been hindering the grant. Similarly, comparing multiple versions of theses to identify areas of and types of significant development over time can aid the thesis-writing process.

■ Program Administration

Corpus analysis of student work can help with writing program administration, as Danielle Wetzel et al. (2021) note: "Those of us who lead writing programs continue to press toward using writing analytics to better understand how to design, deliver, and assess instruction" (p. 292). Corpus analysis of pedagogical and departmental materials can help administrators analyze, assess, evaluate, and improve pedagogy consistently and continuously (Sonnenberg et al., 2022).

Corpus-assisted studies about trends in student writing can tell us something about the changing nature of student work and the kinds of pedagogical practices that can effectively reach students. We can also learn something about our values in the process, by discovering how corpora of student writing or our own teaching materials tell us something about how our academic programs are oriented to particular outcomes. For example, Dylan Dryer's corpus analytic work studying scoring rubrics (2013) reveals insights about how the instruments that instructors develop for assessing writing shift attention to qualities taken to be inherent in the writing and the writers, rather than situationally derived qualities. In other words, corpus analysis can help us better understand the instruments and analytics that we use to gain perspective on programmatic pedagogical choices.

Corpus analysis is an ideal tool for large-scale assessment of student work emerging from a program, and findings from that assessment can lead to insights into how to design and deliver pedagogy. For example, Wetzel et al. (2021) demonstrate a textual tool named DocuScope Classroom that allows a wide range of tasks:

> Programs can make claims about particular curricular goals and align those goals with in-class instruction. We believe this approach facilitates a reconceptualization of assessment as both rhetorical and genre-based, but also as formative for instructional design, informing the vertical integration of writing skills across a curriculum as well as course-level instruction, for both academic and professional writing tasks. (p. 293)

DocuScope allows for easy comparison of documents and sections of documents. Students and teachers can use this tool to understand the rhetorical choices in student writing; students can use it to formatively analyze their own writing choices in comparison to others' choices, while teachers can use the tool to assess and visualize aspects of students' written work. Once lexical items and rhetorical choices have been identified, teachers and administrators can assess whether the students, the assignments, and the curricula work together to produce strong writing outcomes. This type of tool can be used in technical communication classrooms and programs just as Wetzel et al. imagine it:

> From a bird's-eye view, we can bridge the gap between university and workplace writing by mapping genre features according to their rhetorical purpose and function rather than their lexico-grammatical structure. Explicitly teaching rhetorical patterns across a variety of genres, through data-informed visualizations from DocuScope Classroom, may prime students to see relationships between writing tasks they encounter, enabling meaningful learning transfer (p. 319–320).

While specialized tools such as DocuScope Classroom are invaluable for certain types of analysis and outputs (such as visualizations), basic tools can also provide program-level insights. For example, Thomas Peele (2018) used a corpus analysis of 548 student essays as an "assessment tool, providing a microscopic view of a limited number of rhetorical moves. . . . As a result of our study, we hoped to be able to create assignments for research essays that responded directly to the patterns that we saw in our students' essays" (p. 79). Comparing the rhetorical moves students actually made to the moves taught to them from *They Say/I Say* allowed the teachers to assess the students' uptake of tasks at a programmatic level and create curriculum that responded to what they found. Thus, corpus analysis of classroom work that leads to programmatic assessment can work at a variety of levels of scale, complexity and experience: Peele noted that the researchers had "little prior experience with corpus analysis" and used the main functions of a standard corpus analysis tool (ANTCONC) (p. 79).

Other content types could be productively studied for administrative purposes. Web content from technical communication programs' websites could be analyzed to identify ways that programs position themselves in relation to their universities, communities, theories, practices, or other concerns. Analysis of the types of news stories or updates that programs present on their websites may reflect pedagogical or administrative priorities. Analysis of terminology in frequently offered class names can shed light on areas of growth in the field and potential development for individual programs.

With ethical considerations in mind, corpus analysis can be a productive tool for student invention, classroom assessment, programmatic assessment, and curricular development. Ideally, students can take what they have learned about corpus analysis in their studies with them to the workplace. One of our reasons for writing this book is to encourage this sort of work in technical communication programs. While the field has matured, the area of program administration is one that has not taken advantage of corpus analysis work to the same extent as first year writing has (as evidenced by the comparatively smaller number of studies in technical communication on the topic). Program administration is a place where corpus analysis can help the field continue to grow and mature.

◼ Practice

Corpus analysis can also aid technical communicators in the workplace, both in their daily work and research. Whether the aim is to understand a mountain of user input, customer queries, focus group answers, or usability test feedback, corpus analysis methods offer ways to draw meaningful conclusions and get work done. Technical communication practice is constantly evolving. Writers search for ways to gather better feedback and incorporate that feedback more thoroughly and consistently. Managers consistently seek improved efficiency and more effective oversight. These motives can be met through corpus analytic reflection on existing practice. This reflection can start in prominent places, such as trends in user feedback; considering less prominent places, such as language that facilitates efficient translation and more effective localization, may also be productive. Below, we demonstrate three areas where corpus analysis could offer benefits: user feedback, content management, and technical editing.

◼ User Feedback

Consider user feedback, a common part of technical communication (Swarts, 2018). Technical communicators can handle many thousands of units of user feedback solicited from online forms and forums. Tom Johnson (2020) notes that "user champion," a person who gathers user feedback from a variety of sources and presents the user's opinions to the engineers, is an increasingly common role that technical communicators take on. Although the promise of starting a user community and crowd-sourcing some aspects of documentation and revision seem enticing, it is easy to get lost in the sheer amount of user feedback generated. Using corpus analysis to examine the patterns of user contributions may help reveal systematic ways that users make contributions to documentation projects. Upon learning what those modes of contribution are, for example, one could develop tools to better support those kinds of reader engagement. Corpus analysis is well-suited to surfacing trends from a variety of sources, so organizations interested in studying their user communities can use corpus analysis to make the job of finding trends from users easier. Corpus analysis also provides a way of quantifying the severity of concerns to engineers (e.g., "51 users from three sources of feedback are concerned about problem X").

◼ Content Management

Content managers have enormous amounts of digital text under their control, as some organizations maintain vast internal content management systems containing decades of carefully developed and curated content. Content strategists and web content management experts tell organizations how to get a grip on all of their content, inventory it, and know what is covered and how (e.g., Hackos, 2002; Halvorson & Rach, 2012). Content strategists developing content models may also make good use of corpus analysis. Content modeling is about finding what content goes together and what should be separate, and, in particular, what elements connect the content that should be organized together (Andrews, 2020) and these kinds of content patterns may not be apparent without examining many examples of similar kinds of connections. This work will take a detailed approach from someone capable of reflecting analytically on the findings, because fully algorithmic matching is not enough to create effective categories. As Michael Andrews notes:

> Humans decide taxonomies—even when machines provide assistance finding patterns of similarity. Users of taxonomies need to understand the basis of similarity. No matter how experienced the taxonomist or sophisticated the text analysis, the basis of a taxonomy should be explainable and repeatable ideally. Machine-driven clustering approaches lack these qualities. (2020, n.p.)

Corpus analysis offers a way to identify explainable and repeatable bases of taxonomies whose significance can then be validated through close qualitative analysis.

Technical Editing

Technical editors also can use corpus analysis in their work with large amounts of data. Johnson (2020) notes, "as an editor, you might also check to see how the content compares to the competitor's content. For example, does the content cover the same topics as the competitor's docs?" (n.p.). Comparing content across two large sets of text to identify points of comparison or similarity is a task to which corpus analysis is well-suited. Technical communicators dealing with API documentation may use corpus analysis tools to compare and contrast aspects of APIs that change over time. Johnson notes that

> [a]nother non-writing role we play is as an editor who makes the content align with style guides and standards, who figures out whether the content uses the right terms, whether it aligns with industry best practices and style guides, and so on. (n.p.)

Identifying varied term use is an ideal use case for corpus analysis because corpus analysts can assess large amounts of content for questions like these.

Similarly, one might employ corpus analytic techniques to examine subtle differences in documentation that affect how the content is translated and localized in different global markets. A comparison of documentation that has been successfully localized versus unsuccessfully localized might reveal patterns of language use that could be associated with known constraints on localization processes. The result of such an analysis could more readily lead to the kinds of comprehensive guides which inform practical technical practice (e.g., Kohl, 2008). These examples demonstrate several potential organizational uses of corpora and corpus analysis; many more areas of technical communication practice that can benefit from corpus analysis.

To reiterate our point made prior to this review of potential areas for reflective scholarship, our aim has not been to identify areas of technical communication most in need of corpus approaches. Rather, our aim has been to argue that trends in ongoing areas of scholarship, teaching, and professional practice are already leaning into questions that reflect a maturation of the field, as well as a need for the kind of scope and vision that corpus tools can provide.

The specific ends that researchers, teachers, administrators, and students of technical communication will seek with corpus analysis tools will vary, but the tools each help point toward an overarching end: turning large amounts of text into insights that can positively affect the processes of writing for individuals. We will spend the rest of the book outlining in more detail the ideas, tools, and processes that allow people to conduct corpus analysis.

■ Chapters

In this section, we outline the chapters of the book. Each chapter illustrates how a step in corpus analysis research connects to practice and research in technical communication. We will cover initial ideas, tool use, data processing data, reporting findings and more.

Chapter 2 explains the basic terms, techniques, and concepts of corpus analysis. We cover the main necessary elements of corpus analysis, walk through some techniques of analysis (such as keyness and collocation), and explain the theoretical assumptions of corpus analysis. In each of these points, we tie the techniques back to their use in technical communication research. This chapter shows how the analytic functions of corpus analysis align with the questions of technical communication. It also lays the groundwork for future chapters.

Chapter 3 considers how to form research questions for corpus analysis research. We offer an overview of the steps needed to frame issues of technical communication research or practice as questions that can be addressed through corpus analytic techniques. The chapter first discusses the affordances and constraints of qualitative, hand-coded approaches to technical communication research and contrasts those with the affordances and constraints of corpus analytic techniques. We take the concept of a "theoretical framework" to discuss how to use literature and our experiences to frame research questions that are answerable through corpus analytic means. The balance of the chapter provides an overview of question types that one can ask of corpora. We review research in technical communication that attempts to answer similar kinds of research questions through corpus analytic means in order to highlight different methodological decisions that researchers might make. We conclude with a discussion of how to answer these research questions by relying on corpora to approach the issues inductively or deductively.

Chapter 4 takes up the issue of corpus construction. Just as a good research project requires careful selection of research participants and/or thoughtful and purposeful selection of texts for close analysis, corpora must also be cultivated with questions of representativeness, validity, and reliability in mind. The chapter first grapples with the issue of how to create a representative corpus and what representativeness means. We then discuss ways of building corpora through automated and non-automated ways, including the associated ethical issues. The chapter concludes with additional preparatory steps one might make to a corpus to prepare it for analysis, including annotation.

Chapter 5 explains technical aspects of the research infrastructure needed to complete corpus analysis. The chapter gives a brief overview of the capabilities of several corpus analysis tools and information on how to select the appropriate tool for a research project. We turn then to the process and ethics of gathering and sampling data. We conclude with a discussion of how to answer these research questions by relying on corpora to approach the issues inductively or deductively.

Chapter 6 offers a reflective demonstration of corpus analysis techniques applied to a question in contemporary technical communication scholarship: writing style in topic-based documentation. We present the chapter as a stand-alone study of technical communication that benefits from tackling questions at the level of whole corpora. In contextualizing and setting up the study, we reflect in a meta-discursive way about the nature of the problem (i.e., what is the style of topic-based writing) and why it is best answered through a comparison of corpora. We then walk readers through the analytic design, including meta commentary about methodological choices. We carefully and explicitly draw findings from the two study corpora: topic-based and book-based writing. We demonstrate how to carry out the analysis and document the findings with evidence drawn from the corpora.

Chapter 7 concludes the book. We turn our attention to concrete steps that can help develop corpus analysis as a legitimate and mature tool for knowledge creation in the field. We then discuss issues regarding field-level resources to ensure that the relatively challenging startup cost of corpus analysis can be offset by strategic moves as a field that would provide communal resources for supporting this kind of research. We close by arguing that the next step in the maturation process for technical communication is to further enter large conversations about interdisciplinary and transdisciplinary research problems via the legitimating force of big data (via corpus analysis).

Ultimately, the goal of the book is to build on the field's existing work in corpus analysis and present the currently specialized study of corpus analysis to a larger audience of technical communication scholars. This book is intended as a guide that helps scholars imagine how their work could be enhanced or aided by corpus analysis. This book does that by offering readers a window into the different steps of the process in corpus analysis. Each of these topics in the upcoming chapters can be studied in much greater length elsewhere: omnibus sources such as the 754–page Routledge Handbook of Corpus Linguistics (O'Keeffe

& McCarthy, 2022) offer a wider array of concepts, while specialized resources like *What's In a Word-list?: Investigating Word Frequency and Keyword Extraction* (Archer, 2009b) or *Corpus Annotation: Linguistic Information from Computer Text Corpora* (Garside et al., 2013) offer much more depth on individual topics.

2. Assumptions, Approaches, and Techniques of Corpus Analysis

Methodologies give researchers ways of investigating and interpreting the world, and each methodology includes assumptions and approaches. Assumptions offer theoretical reasoning that underpins the method, informing and validating the method's approaches. The approaches encompass techniques by which researchers choose to conduct the analysis and discover the findings. Understanding the assumptions of a method allows researchers to know whether the method is suitable for the purposes of each individual project. Understanding the approaches will let the researcher know where to start once the project has been deemed suitable. Understanding the techniques will allow a researcher to get to work analyzing data once an approach has been chosen.

In this chapter, we will discuss some assumptions of corpus analysis, including those related to lexical significance, quantification, size, degrees of generalizability, and reflection. We will then show how these assumptions underpin the approaches of corpus analysis, including lexicography, grammar, discourse, and register. We will then explain analytic techniques of corpus analysis in light of the assumptions and approaches, including frequency, proportional representation, dispersion, collocation, lemmatization, corpora comparison, and keyness. Finally, we briefly mention some advanced analytic methods that can be pursued after analysts collect initial findings from the techniques above. Along the way, we offer examples of research questions to show how these ideas connect with and further the work of technical communication. This overview of assumptions, approaches, and techniques form a basis of knowledge from which all corpus analyses emerge. It will also be a good context for understanding corpus analysis study design, which is the subject of Chapters 3 through 5.

Assumptions of Corpus Analysis

In this section, we discuss what we call "assumptions" of corpus analysis. We use "assumptions" to mean the concepts that underpin corpus analysis. Using corpus analysis means assuming that these concepts are true to at least some extent. These theoretical pillars form the basis of corpus analysis, and corpus analysts rely on these concepts when explaining their methods. Thus, understanding these concepts is necessary for corpus analysts.

Assumption 1: Lexical Significance

Corpus analysis assumes that the words used in discourse matter. For example, a writer's word choices tell us about the work that the writer is doing to develop meaning and elicit understanding in readers. Likewise, collections of texts with similar patterns of word use tell us something about the work that those texts do. Corpus analysis is a way to understand these functions of texts.

Words signify concepts intrinsically, as each word has at least one meaning. Words contribute at least this intrinsic meaning to the overall meaning of the sentence in which they exist.[1] While each word does not include the totality of meaning of the sentence that the word exists in, each word contributes to the meaning. Similarly, each word contributes to the meaning of the overall text, if only in a small way. This assumption stands in contrast to the idea that full sentences, paragraphs, or arguments must be evaluated to understand meaning.

Lexical significance further implies that variation in word usage is not random. Authors make meaningful choices about which words to use, and those choices are revealed to us through corpus analysis. While the reasons behind the choices of words cannot be immediately revealed through quantitative analysis, the analyst can assume that the author chose, specifically, to repeat or not repeat words in an attempt to make meaning.

Thus, corpus analysis assumes lexical significance: that individual words of discourse matter in their distinctive meaning and repeated use, revealing valid aspects of and suggesting further areas of inquiry into the texts including those words.

▌ Assumption 2: Quantification

Corpus analysis methods assume that quantification of language reveals meaningful features of language use for the analyst to contextualize.

Instead of reducing the value of words by turning them into values, quantification can help researchers identify the importance of certain words in a text. A word appearing with great frequency suggests that at least one meaning of the repeated word is valuable to the content of the message in some way. For example, if the word "hazard" appears more often than "mitigation" in a set of reports on a local power plant, these word choices suggest that the documents offer more frequent information about a hazard than mitigation. However, the quantitative assessment of words does not suggest why the hazard is mentioned more often than mitigation. The document may detail hazards and suggest mitigation as a result; alternatively, the author of the report may dispute that a hazard exists and therefore does not often mention mitigation. Further quantitative or qualitative analysis may reveal the significance(s) of hazard versus mitigation in the document.

---

1.   "At least" in the sense that many other ways of making and activating meaning with printed words exist. The author may be using words intertextually, such as in this footnote. The readers bring their own, extrinsic meanings to the words of the text. Communities of practice may also bring extrinsic meanings to the text and have different connotations for what the denoted words mean. The problems of textual reception are myriad.

Some further analysis types, relying on quantification, can consist of looking at words nearby the frequently occurring word, reading instances of the frequently occurring words in sentence contexts, and qualitatively creating collections of words with similar meanings. Each of these methods can contribute to the understanding of individual words in a text. For example, finding a cluster of words surrounding a single topic, like helping users—such as "help," "user," "audience," and "usability"—in a corpus of technical communication research article abstracts suggests that research abstracts including those words may be about helping users in some way (Carradini, 2020). Further research on the topic(s) suggested by a quantified collection of words may result in insights about the overall text that included those words.

Quantitative findings drawn from large corpora also offer insights into trends that researchers may not identify on close reading. By identifying patterns of functional language use, we can discover more nuanced ways of understanding the significance of nearby content words. For example, the presence of hedging words (e.g., "might," "seem," "appears," "perhaps") or attitude markers (e.g., "astoundingly," "surprisingly," "expectedly," "characteristically") reveal how words instruct readers or listeners on how to engage with the content (e.g., Hyland, 2005). Returning to an earlier example, frequent use of the term "hazard" may be ambiguous on its own, but if the word hazard is accompanied by words like "might" or "may" we might suspect that the likelihood of a hazard is being downplayed.

These quantitative trends do not immediately offer a full context for each occurrence of the word. The numbers must be interpreted. For example, Boettger and Wulff (2014) report on the keywords "this" and "be" from a corpora of student technical writing. The raw numbers of occurrences of "this" and "be" do not tell a meaningful story on their own, but when the authors place "this" and "be" in the context of a pedagogically-oriented grammatical concern regarding the (un)attended *this*, the quantification of the words takes on meaning from the context of the pedagogical idea. The authors found that "[s]tudent writers used *this* + 'be' / 'mean' clusters to perform metadiscoursal functions of summarizing or commenting on previous statements" (p. 132), which gives context to what these two words might be doing together.

The patterns of language use discovered via quantitative analysis enable researchers to surface areas and texts that could profitably be researched further via close reading. For example, understanding the dispersion of a term in a chronologically-ordered corpus can tell a researcher whether a word is increasing or declining in use over time. The discovery that a word is declining in use over time is only meaningful if we have first developed an understanding of what the corpus represents and how that corpus fits into real-world concerns. For example, a decline in the word "computer" in a set of chronologically-ordered software documentation has a different meaning than a decline of the word "responsibility" in chronologically-ordered corporate reports. These sorts of trends are not easily discovered in close reading studies, but close reading of the patterns identified via quantitative analysis can provide insight about the language practices the corpus represents. Thus, corpus analysis becomes a sort of sampling method for qualitative analysis; a way of quickly determining what may be valuable to the research and what is not. Corpus analysis does not lose sight of the meaning of the texts; instead, it helps highlight meaning, identifying elements in a large corpus of texts that could influence and even help contextualize a reader's understanding of what any one text in that corpus means.

Researchers conducting corpus analysis can contextualize quantitative results several ways. One way is through qualitative analysis. Researchers conducting qualitative close examination of words and texts surfaced by corpus analysis can develop numerical findings into contextually-aware studies. A common move in corpus analysis consists of identifying a frequently appearing word in a corpus and reading the sentences that the frequently occurring word appears in. This approach, called "key word in context" or KWIC, allows the quantitative analysis of frequency to turn directly to the qualitative analysis of words in their original context. From this reading of the words in their original locations within sentences and paragraphs, researchers can develop a sense of how a frequently occurring word is used and what those uses may mean for the research questions at hand. Drawing out examples to illustrate exemplary usages of the frequently occurring word is another qualitative step forward.

Researchers can also provide context for quantitative, hypothesis-driven studies by situating the results in the literature or professional conditions that give rise to the study and by explaining their significance in prose. For example, researchers could answer a question about the level of informality displayed in effective resolution of technical issues via a social media platform by confirming the existence in the corpus of certain types of online slang from the helpdesk employee. The researchers may find that certain types of slang exist in successful resolutions but not in unsuccessful resolutions, making the quantitative confirmation of the slang meaningful. In some cases, quantitative confirmation can be enough to answer the research questions and productively build knowledge about technical communication concerns. Where it is not, quantification can lead to other findings (quantitative or qualitative) that help further contextualize the initial quantitative results.

Ultimately, quantification offers a way to identify findings and areas for further study. After this first step, these findings can be developed into meaningful, contextually-understood answers to research questions in a variety of ways.

◼ Assumption 3: Size

Corpus analysis assumes that analysts can answer questions about texts by researching large amounts of text. Thus, corpus analysis addresses a problem that practitioners and academic technical communicators can encounter: a limited ability to scale up research when scale is desired.

Size allows recurrent patterns of words and phrases to appear that would not be easily seen in a small amount of texts. For example, if only four of 100 documents of a genre type feature a particular theme or element, this generic feature being present in 4 percent of documents might not be noted as particularly important or consistent. However, if that trend persists in four percent of 100,000 documents, then the 4,000 documents which present that specific theme or element may reflect a relevant trend that was not visible or prominent at a small scale.

Thus, looking through large numbers of texts can indicate areas of *individual* texts that are ripe for further analysis; finding a frequent word or set of words in a corpus can direct the researcher to investigate the location of those words in each document where they appear. Findings discovered in these meaningful areas can then point the way forward for practical actions and interventions. This concept was demonstrated by Peele (2018), who conducted a study of first-year writing students that

> served as an assessment tool, providing a microscopic view of a limited number of rhetorical moves across a large corpus of student essays. As a result of our study, we hoped to be able to create assignments for research essays that responded directly to the patterns that we saw in our students' essays. (p.79)

The size of the corpus gave a meaningful sense of student writing patterns that Peele and colleagues could respond to.

However, it is not just the absolute or relative frequency counts that matter—the size of the data set matters equally. A moderate-strength pattern of usage in a large data set and a strong pattern of usage in a small data set may not result in the same levels of certainty. For example, a positive trend found in a corpus of student papers from a single teacher may mean that the teacher's pedagogy is effective for that measure, but a positive trend found in a corpus of student papers from a whole program may mean that curricular goals are being reached across multiple teachers. To illustrate, a study by Djuddah A. Leijen (2017) used an analysis of peer review comments at scale to determine, quantitatively, which kind of peer review response best predicted meaningful student revisions. Without a large number of texts to examine, the model of fit between reviewer comments and student revisions might not have been as meaningful. Given this example, reporting corpus sizes and the makeup of the corpus alongside word and phrase frequency counts contributes to the understanding of corpus analysis findings.

Beyond the technical assumptions of size, corpus analysis offers practical assumptions regarding size. The size of corpora in corpus analysis offers researchers the ability to study amounts of texts that are impractical or even impossible for qualitative researchers. As Graham et al. (2015) noted in a study of 70,000 units of analysis across 5,000 pages of the U.S. Food and Drug Administration's Oncologic Drugs Advisory Committee Meeting transcripts:

> No straightforward rhetorical analysis, genre analysis, qualitative
> coding exercise, or similar approach common to technical commu-
> nication research is capable of capturing the full scope of this data
> set or making a meaningful comparison across different meetings
> with differential stakeholder representation. (p. 89)

The authors' statistical genre analysis varies from corpus analysis in certain ways, yet their approach and corpus analysis both address the same concern: "Big data is quickly becoming coin of the realm in academia. In disciplines ranging from physics to policy studies, there is a growing emphasis on new techniques to explore and manage vastly large and complex data sets" (p. 70). Corpus analysis allows technical communicators ways of exploring and managing large amounts of text.

While reading at scale is a different way of reading than reading a single document beginning to end, it is a way of reading that privileges what many texts have to say about an issue (Miller & Licastro, 2021, p. 9). One primary goal of corpus analysis is to identify meaningful aspects of individual texts across larger sets of documents than could be manually assessed. Scale does not result in a loss of meaning for the findings, so long as those findings are interpreted within the context of the texts themselves.

Assumption 4: Degrees of Generalizability

Making more observations in a bigger data set to find patterns of usage will yield degrees of generalizability. For example, analyzing 10 versions of a software's documentation can offer insights that could be further investigated for usefulness. Doing a corpus analysis of all of a software company's documentation from 2010–2020 allows researchers to claim findings as generalizable for that time period.

The size of a corpus also assists with generalizability. In a corpus that is sufficiently large, it can be more difficult to find consistent strong patterns of language use than in smaller sets of documents. Patterns that are strong enough to become visible amid all the potential patterns of a large corpus have a strong claim to generalizability in the corpus, but the right to make such a claim relies on the researcher having made careful and reflective choices when compiling the corpus.

As a result of potential comprehensiveness and strength of patterns, findings derived from large amounts of data can validate findings from smaller sets of data. For example, researchers investigating different types of language found in effective and ineffective citizen petitions could identify findings in a small set of legal petitions from Arizona over the period 1999–2020. These findings could be validated by assessing a comprehensive set of Arizona petitions over that time to ascertain if the original findings are present in the full set. The findings could then be considered generalizable for the conditions surrounding those Arizona petitions and instructive for future petitions with the same or similar conditions (such as no new laws being passed to change the nature of petitions).

Corpus analysis can also support making generalizable claims across multiple corpora but doing so requires careful attention to the data that goes into the corpus (see Chapter 4). Even then, the conditions of discourse production represented by the corpus might make claims of bounded generalizability more appropriate. For example, crowdfunding platforms and the corpora of funding campaigns available on them each present unique conditions for discourse. Gary Dushnitsky and Markus A. Fitza (2018) found that "actors associated with success in a given platform do not replicate to the other platforms" (p. 1). This means that findings from a corpus of 320,000 Kickstarter campaigns may be generalizable to Kickstarter campaigns of that time period but are not generalizable to types of crowdfunding proposals outside of Kickstarter, such as on the crowdfunding platform IndieGoGo.

Some scholars are skeptical about claims of generalizability. In fact, many qualitative analyses claim that findings are true only for the local conditions covered by the research and does not attempt to generalize because every condition is different. However, as findings withstand the scrutiny of multiple observations, they acquire truth value that seems more certain than what is obtainable from fewer observations of fewer data points. Whether corpus-based observations have a higher truth value depends, of course, on the validity and representativeness of one's corpus design (see Chapter 4).

Although some scholars may be unconvinced by arguments for the predictive power of generalizable results, they may be convinced by an argument that changes the scope of the generalization. Corpora can give a comprehensive look at a local condition. Qualitative and quantitative analysis can argue for the existence of a local phenomenon, while corpus analysis can then locate examples of that phenomenon and test for the persistence of the phenomena throughout the corpus. Thus, the generalizable nature of data (especially when comprehensive sets are used to form a corpus) can support local conditions instead of making a larger case for generalizability across locations. This approach could be valuable in program/departmental research, as administrators and researchers can support qualitative or quantitative claims with corpus analysis findings that reflect the same or similar findings over a whole range of documents relevant to the organization.

Corpus analysis can also be conducted with sets of texts that do not approach generalizability. Researchers must understand the amount of data they are analyzing in relation to the full set, and not claim generalizability when the data is not large enough to do so.

▌ Assumption 5: Reflection

Because corpus analysis assumes the need to explain patterns of word usage in a corpus, corpus analysis also assumes self-aware reflection in research. Working with corpora is a complex process that requires many decisions along the way before arriving at and interpreting results. Before starting the analysis, researchers must make reasoned, self-aware decisions about the questions they want to ask (Chapter 3), the corpus they want to find or build (Chapter 4), and the kind of analytic approach to take (Chapter 5). In the process of conducting an analysis, additional self-awareness is required to make good decisions about the act of analysis itself: including or excluding texts from a corpus, setting large or small collocation windows, selecting cut-off points in the data when choosing topics for further analysis, and choosing statistical measures. Each of these choices has effects on the outcomes of the research. Corpus analysis assumes that these decisions will need to be made by the analyst. Thus, the analyst must make and then report the choices made when developing a corpus analysis study.

■ Approaches to Analysis

With these five assumptions in mind, we can consider how they underpin approaches in corpus analysis. Corpus analysis supports analytic inquiries regarding lexicography, grammar, discourse, and register (Biber et al., 2000). These layers of analysis can be thought of as a sliding scale from the more objective, grammatical units (e.g., nouns, indexicals) to more interpretative, but still trackable, units like phrases used across many instances of the same type of situation (Swales, 2011). Because the goal of corpus analysis is to quickly analyze more content than could reasonably be read and analyzed manually, the first two layers of analysis (lexicography and grammar) are primarily quantitative. As mentioned earlier, these quantitative assessments can provide answers to research questions or work as steppingstones to further inquiry. After using lexicography or grammatical analysis to identify areas for further inquiry, researchers can use more interpretative types of analysis, such as those associated with discourse or register analysis.

Our aim below is to explain at a high level the kinds of analyses supported by corpus analysis. In Chapter 3, we discuss how these analytic approaches can be and have been taken up by scholars in our and adjacent fields.

■ Approaches One and Two: Lexicography and Grammar

The first two approaches we will discuss are the lexical and grammatical approaches. The most basic approach is lexical, or word, analysis. While lexical significance and quantification are assumptions of corpus analysis, lexical approaches to corpus analysis do not advance beyond the level of the word. A research question concerning whether more nominals were used in topic-based or book-based documentation would result in a lexical approach to corpus analysis, but by itself it would not provide much additional insight about why. Frequency counts of words in a corpus is a way of doing lexicographical analysis; if frequency counts answer the research question, then no further approach is needed except the lexical approach. Questions such as "what are the main technical concepts discussed in these reports?" "what schools of thought have been brought to bear on this idea?" or "what topics have our engineering meetings been most concerned with over the last year, according to all of the meeting minutes?" could be answered via review of lexical results.

Grammatical approaches build upon lexical approaches by looking at syntactic relationships between words. Looking at words in prepositional phrases, identifying predicates of sentences, or looking at subject/verb relationships in a corpus reveals more complex language phenomena and allows researchers to assess the semantic work that the language is doing. Some research requires only results from lexical or grammatical approaches to answer questions.

One tactic that scholars have employed to operationalize lexical and grammatical approaches is in the tactic of "distant reading." Distant reading seeks a limited understanding of each individual text as a way to understand the corpus as a whole. For example, understanding that every document from a corpus of websites contains the word *liability* suggests something about the corpus as a whole; the corpus is likely related to the concept of liability in some way. Derek N. Mueller (2019) employed distant reading as a way for writing scholars to visualize their academic field, using large amounts of data to identify trends and significant concepts within the field. Mueller offers distant reading (along with *thin description*, the opposite of *thick description*) as a way to "foster primary, if tentative and provisional, insights into . . . network sense—incomplete but nevertheless vital glimpses of an interconnected disciplinary domain focused on relationships that define and cohere widespread scholarly activity" (p. 3). Many sorts of corpora can be profitably analyzed with "primary, if tentative and provisional" insights, especially as a first look into the data.

Approaches Three and Four: Discourse and Register

Discourse and register analysis use the results of lexical and grammatical approaches as a way of identifying areas that repay further study at the discourse or register level (Archer, 2009a). A discourse approach is concerned with the function of words in their context of use. Researchers seek to understand how words do work within a document and contribute to the document's identity as a contribution of a particular kind of speech act (Gee, 2005). Discourse analysts could seek to understand how isolated passages within a document function by assessing which words are used frequently and in association with what other words. Another way of looking at the discourse of a document is to understand what the corpus (and thus, what its constituent documents) are *about*. Identifying high frequency words, evenly-dispersed words, or other word use patterns suggests what kind of discourse that corpus represents.

A register approach builds on a discourse approach and seeks to understand how words and their associated discourse patterns are used consistently across many instances of the same type of situation.[2] While a register approach can be operationalized in many ways, we highlight one technique of a register approach here as an example: move analysis. Seeing the same types of words used in the same types of arguments over many documents in a similar situation constitutes a "move" (Swales, 2011), or a distinctive way of participating in a discourse, within a register. Move analysis is a profitable technique of a register approach to identify key patterns that are successful or unsuccessful in making arguments. It has been extensively used to study academic research texts, such as introductions to journal articles. It has also been used to study the moves of such disparate genres as job application letters (Henry & Roseberry, 2001), birthmother letters (Upton & Cohen, 2009), and e-commerce pitches (internet group buying deals; Lam, 2013). Thomas A. Upton and Mary Ann Cohen's (2009) analysis of birthmother letters ("letters written by prospective adoptive parents to expectant mothers considering adoption plans for their unborn children," p. 590) also identified moves and successful strategies within moves, using corpus analysis to identify words and phrases that were more common in successful letters than unsuccessful letters. They found that successful letters used the phrases "our child" and "our baby" more than unsuccessful letters, reasoning that: "By more frequently using 'our child' and 'our baby' as they talk about what their life is and will be like, the letter writers help the expectant mother more easily envision her child in a particular environment, and she can more easily see a couple's intentions" (p. 597). Corpus analysis can help researchers conduct move analysis beyond identifying repeated words that indicate typical moves.

Grouping words into categories can also help analysts with move analysis. Phoenix W. Lam (2013) identified 13 moves within pitches for internet group buying deals and characterized the types of discourse within the pitches: "Although online group buying deals are predominantly promotional, they also show a blend of informative, social, regulatory and instructional discourse" (p. 26). After Alex Henry and Robert L. Roseberry (2001) found eleven moves in job application letters, they also found that one move, "Promoting the Candidate," could be done via multiple strategies: "listing relevant skills, abilities; stating how skills, abilities were obtained; listing qualifications; naming present job; and predicting success" (p. 160). Thus, researchers can conduct various types of detailed move analysis via a register approach to corpus analysis. Discourse and register approaches often require building on a lexical and grammatical approaches via a second stage of

---

2.   Register and *genre* are differing concepts that surround a similar idea: people use language in consistent ways in specific repeated situations. To oversimplify a long discussion: register focuses on how words recur in situations, while genre (especially rhetorical genre studies) is concerned with what common features of language (words, phrases, ideas, structures, formatting, et al.) may be found in the breadth of responses that effectively fit the recurrent situation. Consider Swales (1990).

corpus-assisted close reading. After using lexical or grammatical findings to surface items and to identify areas of further interest, the researcher can give the texts that include those items further qualitative attention in the indicated areas. Placing findings into their context using discourse or register approaches allows the researcher to report examples, explain concepts, and answer complex research questions.

■ Techniques

While technical communication researchers may pursue questions using all four approaches of corpus analysis research, lexical and grammatical approaches to analysis are likely to be the beginning steps. The next few sections cover key techniques that can help.

▓ Frequency

Frequency (sometimes "raw frequency" or "absolute frequency") is the number of times a word or phrase appears in a corpus. It is the bedrock of corpus analysis. Questions like "Do we mention Version 2.0 or Version 3.0 more in our documentation?" are answerable by determining the raw frequency of each term in the corpus. Raw frequency data can sometimes answer questions on its own, but it is a blunt assessment that lacks nuance. More detailed techniques can often shed more light on topics than raw frequency alone. Still, raw frequency can be useful for identifying the answers to certain types of exploratory, discovery-oriented questions that help researchers better understand what is in a corpus. Many of the approaches below build on the concept of frequency.

▓ Proportional Representation

Proportional representation (also called "relative frequency") expresses frequency as a percentage of the whole set of words (or phrases) in the corpus. The figure may also be represented as the number of occurrences per 10,000 words. A statement of proportional representation might look like "the word 'youth' represents 1.2 percent of this corpus." This type of analysis is a strong indicator of how prominent a word or phrase is in a corpus. Saying that the word *youth* appears 10,157 times in a set of governmental reports is not as valuable as knowing that 1.2 percent of all words (or one out of almost every 100 words) in the corpus are the word *youth*. Further, comparing proportional representation is valuable as well: if 1.2 percent of all words are *youth* but no other word commands more than 0.5 percent, it can be argued that *youth* is a prominent word in the corpus even if the proportional representation appears small. Proportional representation can be useful to compare words to each other within a document. For example, finding that 1.2 percent of the words of a corpus are *youth* while 2.2 percent of the words are *adult* suggests different areas of investigation than *youth* alone, such as possible relationships between the two terms.

Furthermore, proportional representation in the form of "occurrences per 10,000 words" is useful as a way of normalizing proportions in order to compare corpora of different sizes. Analyzing the texts of two different city council meetings to identify argumentative strategies can be challenging if 100 city council meeting transcripts are available for one city and 35 are available for another. Using "occurrences per 10,000 words" to identify shared and differing word use can bring the two corpora closer to a level plane for comparison's sake.

Lemmatization

Lemmatization is a process by which the endings of words are ignored in favor of their root word (the lemma). For example, organize, organized, organization, and organizational all have the lemma of organiz. (This would be reported with an asterisk covering the endings that are removed: organiz*.) Lemmatizing a corpus allows for a more conceptual understanding of the content, as the appearance of a single lemma in multiple forms strengthens the case that the corpus may be about a certain topic or topics depicted in the lemmas.

The lemmatization technique moves slightly afield from strict lexical analysis, as the goal is to not assess each individual form of the word as unique. Instead, the goal is to understand the underlying concerns of the corpus by summing words that share the same lemma. For example, a practitioner may identify from an online corpus comments indicating that users are often talking about a failing software program. The practitioner could lemmatize fail* to identify comments that include the words fail, failure, failing, failed, and fails. Lemmatizing is a technique that can be used with any of the above or below techniques, as frequency of lemmas, dispersion of lemmas, and statistical analysis of lemmas can all prove fruitful for certain types of research questions.

Dispersion

Dispersion analysis (sometimes called "distribution analysis") offers additional contextualization for frequency and proportional representation results. Dispersion tallies the number of documents (or web pages, transcripts, content blocks, etc.) that a word or phrase appears in. This technique allows researchers to identify elements that appear across a wide range of documents in a corpus, giving a finer look at term usage in a corpus than frequency alone. For example, in a corpus of 10,000 user help desk tickets with 900 mentions of the word "error," dispersion analysis can identify whether uses of "error" are dispersed across 825 help desk tickets or if 100 tickets contain all the mentions of the term. This can lead to technical communicators understanding the scope of problems more clearly and allocating their labor more effectively, as they can better decide which problems are most serious or noteworthy.

Seeing how well dispersed a word is throughout a corpus is valuable for avoiding interpretations that skew the importance of that word. For example, imagine that 200 uses of *river* are present in a corpus of transcripts of local news reports on climate change. However, 120 of the uses come from five of the 40 transcripts. The dispersion is heavily skewed toward those five transcripts at the expense of the other 35. It may be that the corpus, which looks like it could be about rivers, is not actually as much about rivers as it seemed at first.

Dispersion does not have to be tallied only via frequency; it can be proportional as well. For example, knowing that the word *confusing* appears in 33 percent of documents in a corpus of user experience reports could be as valuable as knowing the raw number of user experience reports the term appears in. Using proportional dispersion as a comparison also enables analysts to compare corpora of different sizes and to subdivide corpora into proportionally meaningful (if differently sized) contrast groups. For example, corpora can be organized in binary, ordinal, or categorical ways. A binary organizational principle could consist of one corpus split into two sub-corpora, one of pre-1999 reports from a company and one of post-1999 reports of a company. Proportional dispersion could answer questions about whether the pre-1999 or post-1999 reports had proportionally more references to the same word or phrase: a researcher could report "pre-1999 reports used the words we, our, and ours 2 percent of the time, while post-1999 reports used those words 4 percent of the time."

An ordinal organizational strategy could consist of 12 collections of student papers, chronologically ordered by semester. Proportional dispersion analysis could show a trend in usage of a word or group of words over time, as a percentage of the papers. This finding could reveal changing trends in writing concerns such as formality, audience-centered language, accessible language, or plain language. Assessing over time could also reveal trends related to how students respond to the same writing assignments in different conditions, such as before and after implementation of a new set of course outcomes, readings, or teaching approaches.

Finally, a categorical strategy could consist of breaking one corpus into four sub-corpora: groups of reports written with no attribution, written by one person, written by two people, or written by three or more people. This organizational principle would allow for an investigation of the dispersion of terms to discern what type of authorship uses collective words like *we, our*, and *ours* proportionally more frequently.

▌ Collocation

Collocation is a technique that identifies which words frequently appear near a target word or phrase in a corpus. The goal of collocation analysis is to identify quantitative relationships between words that can be further analyzed to understand qualitative relationships between the words. For example, researchers may want to investigate the invention stage of entrepreneurs' writing process. In transcripts of interviews with entrepreneurs, frequency analysis could reveal "our" as a frequently occurring word that may repay further inquiry. Then, collocation analysis could show that "collaborators" frequently appears within five words to the left or right of the word "our." Thus, quantitative analysis establishes the existence of some potential relationship between the words. Further qualitative analysis can elaborate on what type of relationship "our" and "collaborators" may have in the context of invention.

Collocation analysis may also reveal common phrases occurring in a corpus. Continuing an earlier example, a collocation analysis could show that "our" appears in "our collaborators" but also in "our results from collaborators" and "our data reveal to collaborators that . . . " Knowing that "our" and "collaborators" are quantitatively related allows for further qualitative inquiry of entrepreneurs' varied relationship to their collaborators.

For another example, this time from crisis communication: in Seung-ji Baek et al.'s (2013) study of Twitter responses to the 2013 Great East Japan Earthquake, the authors identified "HOUSYA (radiation)" as an important word related to the crisis due to high frequency of use over time (p. 1791). The authors then qualitatively analyzed the words surrounding HOUSYA to build out an analysis of what HOUSYA meant in context: an official governmental Twitter account used scientific terms surrounding HOUSYA, depicting low anxiety about the situation; citizen Twitter users used negative words surrounding emotions and safety around HOUSYA, depicting high anxiety about the event (p. 1793). Similar types of analysis of social media in different crises could lead to further contextualization regarding what a mismatch between governmental approaches and citizen approaches might mean in crisis communication.

▮ Comparing Two Corpora and Keyness

Comparing corpora is often a productive technique as well. When comparing corpora, the corpus under analysis is called the "study corpus" or the "target corpus." The corpus used as the basis of comparison is the "reference corpus." Deciding on a study corpus and a reference corpus requires consideration of the theoretical framework that informs that study (Chapter 4). The salient differences between the study and reference corpus are the analytic contrasts that highlight phenomena of interest in the study corpus.

Any of the previous analysis techniques can be used to compare two corpora. A researcher can compare frequencies, proportional representations, or proportional dispersions across corpora. Understanding how corpora differ quantitatively points to areas for further qualitative analysis in the study corpus.

Comparing two corpora from a single source is often ideal, as the baseline similarity between the corpora makes the differences more meaningful. For example, comparing two corpora of professional tweets may be more helpful for understanding techniques of professional social media use than comparing a corpus of tweets to a corpus of course catalog entries. When two corpora from a single source domain are not available, using reference corpora from adjacent domains is a secondary way forward. Even cross-field corpora can be used effectively to understand certain types of research questions, so long as the researcher understands that not all differences between the corpora will be meaningful.[3]

Certain types of analysis can only be done via two-corpus analysis. Keyness is a valuable technique when looking for the differences between two corpora. Analysts use a corpus analysis research tool to statistically analyze which words are more likely or less likely to appear in a target corpus by comparison to a reference corpus. For example, keyness could help determine what words are more "key" in accessible building codes in relation to generic building codes. *Positive* keyness could show that the word *ramp* is 15 percent more likely to be present in a target corpora about building accessibility than the reference corpus about generic building regulations. *Negative* keyness could suggest that the word *material* is less present in the study corpus than the reference corpus.

■ Further Analysis

Discourse and register analysis require moving from the initial lexical/grammatical layers into further analysis on those findings. Further analysis can be qualitative or quantitative. We begin with qualitative analysis.

■ Second-stage Qualitative Analysis

Qualitative corpus analysis is often focused on the meaning of the language in its context. Qualitative analysis follows an initial round of findings by further examining results identified via frequency, proportional representation, lemmatization, dispersion, collocation, or keyness analyses. The second round of analysis can take the form of any qualitative technique. Choosing an individual item, text, or section as an exemplar of the findings is a common way of extending the research. Close reading of items, sections, or whole texts identified in the corpus as meaningful to the research questions could also further the results. Semantic grouping of items, sections, or topics into categories for further study may also help answer research questions (Carradini, 2020; Gerbig, 2010).

A type of second-stage qualitative analysis related to grouping and specific to corpus analysis is determining "aboutness." "Aboutness" is literally what the corpus is "about," such as a group of forum posts *about* a specific technology, a group of citizen reports *about* a civic issue, or a collection of social media posts *about*

---

3. Scott (2009) finds that for certain types of research, even "obviously absurd (reference corpora) can be plausible indicators of aboutness" (p. 91). Scott compared a corpus of Shakespearean plays against a corpus of contemporary language and yet found meaningful results that could point toward further effective qualitative research.

help-desk inquiries. "Aboutness" is particularly associated with the technique of keyness, as the most unusually frequent words indicate what the target corpora talks about more often than the reference corpora. Other techniques produce findings that help assess what a corpora is "about" as well.

▮ Statistical Analysis

The descriptive statistics of the initial findings from corpus analysis can be further developed by use of inferential statistics. Depending on the organization of the data in a corpus and the questions the researcher is seeking to answer, inferential tests such as chi square analysis, linear regression, logistic regression, and more can be conducted to determine relationships between linguistic elements in the corpora.

If the question a researcher wants to answer has a binary dependent variable, such as "Did grant proposals featuring positively valenced words succeed or fail more often?", binary logistic regression might be applicable to answer this question. If the question concerns an ordinal (or ordered, such as chronological or age-range-related data) output, such as "which historic version of a website corresponded to gendered words most often," logistic regression might help answer that question. Questions concerned with categories, such as plotting the statistical relationship of five different laws to types of words used in them, could use various types of tests (t-tests, ANOVA, among others) to identify further relationships that are statistically significant. Michael P. Oakes (1998/2019) and Vaclav Brezina (2018) each offer book-length treatments of statistics for corpus analysis. Brezina (2018) is an introductory guide that assumes "no prior knowledge of statistics" (p. xvii), while Oakes' book is pitched more as a reference book for those more familiar with statistics (p. xii).

Specialized types of quantitative analysis may reveal insights specific to corpus analysis. Natural Language Processing (NLP) is a computing-heavy area of study related to corpus analysis that can develop corpus findings further. NLP techniques such as topic modeling and dependency parsing can offer researchers unique ways of understanding topics in a corpus and detailed understandings of relationships between words, as Arthurs (2018) demonstrated by applying these techniques to aspects of the texts in the Stanford Study of Writing. Specifically, Arthurs used topic modeling to automate the grouping of related words into associated topics. This categorical approach helped identify 18 distinct topics in a corpus of student writing that featured many topics. Technical communicators could use this topic modeling approach to build on initial corpus findings or as a method to surface documents about certain topics from within a heterogeneous group of texts.

▮ Conclusion

Responsible corpus analysis research starts with understanding the assumptions of corpus analysis: lexical significance, quantification, size, degrees of generalizability, and reflection. From these assumptions grow the layers of corpus analysis: lexical, grammatical, discourse, and register. Lexical and grammatical analysis is primarily quantitative, identifying areas for further research and answering research questions about numerical aspects of words in texts. Register and discourse analysis are primarily qualitative, further investigating initial quantitative findings with a variety of qualitative and quantitative methods. Regardless of whether the researcher stays at the quantitative level or goes on to the qualitative level to answer research questions, the researcher must use analysis techniques that begin at the quantitative level. Some of these techniques are frequency, proportional representation, lemmatization, dispersion, collocation, corpora comparison, and keyness. These assumptions, approaches, and techniques form the theoretical basis of corpus analysis.

From this theoretical basis, analysts can begin to develop corpus analysis projects that best respond to the research questions. Although we have tried to ground these *theoretical* ideas in example research questions, these ideas still can seem a bit abstract. In the next chapter, we will consider the *practical* basis of corpus analysis: the corpus, and how to build it.

3. Developing Questions

Across the previous two chapters, we have introduced corpus analysis as a method that can address questions too large to consider without the perspective afforded by expansive, large-scale analysis of many texts.

This chapter explains how to develop questions that can be addressed through corpus analysis. First, we describe theoretical elements regarding human research capabilities in contrast to use of analytic research tools, such as those employed by corpus analysis. We then discuss how to frame inquiries that can be supported by corpus analysis tools without requiring too much compromise on the objectives of our inquiries. A short overview of questions that people in the field of technical communication have asked and answered with corpus analytic techniques follows. These examples can guide us in developing our own questions.

Research Tools and Their Affordances

We begin this chapter with a philosophical look at the affordances and constraints of tools available to assist in corpus analysis. We use the term affordance in the manner proposed by J. J. Gibson (1986), who linked the idea to situated acts of perception. Within a given setting in which one is motivated to carry out some action, a person will discover the possibilities for taking action in their tools and other resources. The qualities of those tools or resources that lend themselves to the user's purposes are its affordances. Yet the affordances are not inherent in the tools or resources. Instead, users perceive the affordances when motivated to look for them. Corpus analytic tools also have affordances that can be perceived in many settings. The corpus analytic tools discussed in this volume were created and used by linguists for the study of linguistic phenomena, but the tools also afford the discourse-level analysis that is common in writing research.

The term "affordance" acquires its meaning, in part, because of how it has been used in discourse on human-computer interaction. In that research, an "affordance" describes an active relationship between a user and a tool or technology. Supported by a tool or technology, a user senses action possibilities that are available due to the design of the tool (Norman, 1989). In the context of research, these action possibilities go beyond the physical to the cognitive and social (Kaptelinin, 1996). Some tools and technologies extend our cognitive capabilities by extending our senses (McLuhan, 1994). With our enhanced sensory and cognitive abilities, we are better able to complete tasks that we are otherwise not particularly good at doing (e.g., using computer simulations to process variables that predict outcomes for uncertain events).

Tools and technologies for research inquiry further help us by creating external representations of the phenomena we are studying. These external representations then mediate our internal representations that guide closer qualitative examination of cases (Zhang & Patel, 2006). These internal representations aid researchers in seeing those phenomena as meaningful objects within research narratives (Harré, 2002).

Instead of beginning with specialized corpus analysis software tools, it is better to start with intimately familiar research instruments, like our own sense of perception and ability to interpret discourse to infer meaning. As social beings, we have a lived experience of working within discourse. We have developed a fair degree of sophistication at listening to discourse and inferring meaning from what has been spoken or written. Often, the meaning that we infer is grounded in the context where we encounter this discourse. We are able to connect those words and phrases to contexts that give them meaning beyond the denotative meanings associated with the words themselves.

Furthermore, because we experience discourse and text as unfolding over time (e.g., whether in the context of a conversation or in the context of reading a passage in a book), we are able to draw connections between pieces of discourse that are disconnected in space and time (Goody & Watt, 1963). We can connect something that we hear today with something said yesterday or a week ago. Those temporal connections add to our understanding of the words present before us. We can also infer meaning across texts because we are tuned to their inherent intertextual connections (Bakhtin, 1981). We recognize allusions in text because we have encountered passages before, or perhaps because we recognize character archetypes, motifs, or themes that gesture at cultural touchstones (Sapienza, 2007).

The point is that humans are good at inferring meaning from what is absent but implied in the words that we are reading or hearing. Yet software that is designed to look for linguistic traces of discourse will not find what is *not* present in the text. This is one reason why we have relied so heavily on close reading of text for research in writing: it brings us closer to the full nuance of interpretation that the text supports. With enough sustained study, humans might become good at sensing differences within a body of discourse. However, that process of gaining an embodied understanding must begin again when the data set changes. Analytic tools like corpus analysis are effective at helping us make the connection between qualitative interpretative of textual features on a small scale with observable, recurring language patterns that may correlate with those features but be difficult to see over a large body of data.

Consider the work that has been done on DocuScope at Carnegie Mellon (Kaufer & Ishizaki, 1998). Over time and after analyzing volumes of text, DocuScope now has robust dictionaries that describe different rhetorical and grammatical tactics that might be used in different kinds of discourse. As the DocuScope creators argue, these approaches 1) treat small writing decisions as meaningful, 2) make those small choices visible, 3) make decisions about writing while being aware of those small actions, and 4) provide ways for writers to review their writing to make data-informed decisions about how to approach their work. Such a tool effectively enables writers to "develop metacognition" about their writing (Wetzel et al., p. 296). Whereas DocuScope might guide writers to become better at their craft by affording a reflective metacognitive awareness of their own writing, the same computer-assisted techniques can help researchers become similarly reflective about the texts that they study.

Corpus analysis is just such a tool-based, empirical approach to the study of discourse and its pragmatic uses across contexts. When we interpret discourse across contexts, we tap into experiences that underlie our understanding of cognitively and physically remote contexts. Yet those experiences, especially those more remote from our immediate experience, are prone to mistakes. We attempt to correct these mistakes through analytic investigation (James, 2019). Our research tools help us reflect on our experiences, ideally by removing or keeping in check the potential for interpretive bias.

Human perception of discourse is fallible in ways that can be detrimental to certain kinds of research. Given a large enough body of discourse to review and study, human readers lose attention. We get tired and bored and distracted. We miss things, identify things that are not there, misunderstand what we have read, or rely on imprecise or incorrect intuitions about discourse. Studies that rely on human coding of discourse depend critically on measures of second coder reliability (Creswell, 1994; Krippendorff, 2018) to demonstrate that appropriate steps have been taken to mitigate the problems associated with fallible human judgment.

There are also the practical concerns when relying on human judgment of discourse. To begin with, we are slow. Our reading speed is no match for the processing speed of software, setting aside the obvious difference that software is doing more pattern recognition than actual reading and processing. Human readers are also not very good at seeing systematic variation across large sets of discourse.

We are also not very good at recognizing usual or typified uses of language across many instances (Biber et al., 2000). Yet, the very idea of genre as a social act (e.g., Miller, 1984; Spinuzzi, 2003) depends on our ability to recognize such systematic regularities. When it is difficult for human readers to discern these patterns of usage, it will be that much more difficult for them to draw inferences about the associations between those patterns in a large body of discourse: not only if patterns occur with other patterns, but how often and how strongly those patterns are associated. Likewise, readers may be less capable of deciding on an answer to a question about how different bodies of discourse are from one another on the basis of those patterns. These constraints on the human perception of patterns in discourse reveal the benefits of computational approaches such as computational analysis and pattern matching.

Furthermore, there are times when studying discourse requires close attention to language that we do not typically associate with the "message" or "content." Many glue words, such as conjunctions, adverbs, indexicals, modals, and determiners, are easy to overlook because their function is to help tie together concepts, actors, and actions in the discourse. However, those words are often significantly connected to the kind of work that a text or body of discourse is doing (Pennebaker, 2011). If we interpret discourse as making and linking assertions about the world and our experiences of it, the function words are the "conjunctive relations" that link those assertions together and enrich our understanding of the experiences they convey. The function words coordinate assertions, subordinate them, amplify them, modify them, and cast doubt on them.

Related to raw counting, software supporting corpus analysis can also compare data of varying sizes. Whether the source data is in paragraphs, chapters, or a series of sentences, corpus analysis software will produce accurate counts and comparisons across those natural or analyst-selected units of segmentation (e.g., divisions between files, content grouped by topics, etc.). Because these searches and comparisons of the discourse can be automated, the entire analysis can be scaled up or down. The analysis can also be subdivided into different comparison units as the study evolves and new data are added. The sum result is an overview of a large body of discourse that gives some points of quantitative comparison, allowing researchers to determine both the magnitude and significance of patterns located in the data.

Despite these arguments, we hasten to point out that the takeaway is not that human, qualitative interpretation is irredeemably faulty and that machine interpretation is preferred. For one thing, there are clear dangers associated with the perspective that computational interpretations are better for the lack of human interference (Noble, 2018). Walter Ong argues that human interpretation, our hermeneutic approach to language analysis, is needed because while machines are capable of processing digitized content, there is plenty of meaning in discourse that cannot be digitized, such as context, nonverbal information, silence, and uptake (2018). Machines and corpus analytic techniques in particular assist the hermeneutic, interpretive work by processing language patterns that can be digitized, which can then help human readers with interpretation. The tools are worth knowing something about both to take advantage of their affordances, but also to understand how they can shape interpretation.

Asking Questions

Recognizing the affordances and limitations of corpus analysis software is the first step in writing good questions that can take advantage of the software's affordances while articulating clear value that can be added by human interpretation. To summarize those affordances and limitations: first, corpus analysis software is good at answering empirical questions or those that rely on systematic and reliable observations of discourse. Secondarily, we can argue that corpus analysis software is capable of making observations that allow human researchers to make limited inferences about the dispersion of discourse features within a corpus. In other words, the software allows us to make limited inferences about the similarities and differences between corpora that we might want to compare.

Given these affordances, we can classify some of the empirical questions that are answerable by corpus analysis. There are eight question types, which we derive in part from Cheryl Geisler and Jason Swarts (2019):

- **Questions of kind** are definitional and provide insight about what kinds of content make up a corpus.
- **Questions of dispersion** show how evenly or unevenly a discourse or linguistic feature is spread throughout a corpus.
- **Questions of association** show how often two or more linguistic or discursive features appear together (or in each other's absence).
- **Questions of time** show the frequency of discourse, linguistic features, or associations over the amount of time that a corpus elapses.
- **Questions of meaning** are analyses of keywords that compare the expected frequency of terms across corpora in order to provide insights about how corpora differ in meaning.
- **Questions of identity** build upon questions of kind and association, offering pattern interpretation that aims to characterize the purpose that discourse in a corpus represents.
- **Questions of use** draw inferences about how participants in a discourse are using language to interact with each other, with ideas, or with other agents.
- **Questions of convention** draw inferences about systematic use of linguistic patterns to evaluate what they reveal about the discourse and social actions they support.

One way to subdivide these types of questions we might ask is to separate them into questions that provide observations of patterns in a corpus and questions that support inferential thinking on the basis of observed patterns.

◼ Observational Questions

Observational questions ask about qualities of discourse that can be counted. These questions yield tallies of discourse or linguistic features. A researcher's job is to link a countable feature (e.g., modal language) with a qualitative feature worth close interpretation (e.g., hypothetical thinking). Sometimes there may be a direct correspondence between a tallied feature and point of interpretation. At other times, the complexity of the phenomenon under investigation might depend on identifying more than one countable feature to link to a qualitative feature. For example, we might take the presence of third person pronouns and verbs associated with assertions together to indicate a shift in a writer's basis for argumentation.

Questions of kind provide information about observable features of the discourse, what they consist of, and what they look like. For example, imagine reviewing a corpus of talk-aloud protocols from a series of usability tests to understand where and on what tasks users experienced difficulty. We might want to track how often the word "understand" occurs. The task would result in data showing a raw frequency count, as well as information about the relative frequency of the word throughout the corpus, often normalized the expected proportion per 10k words. We could also learn about how thoroughly the word "understand" is spread throughout a corpus by looking at the evenness of its *dispersion* through the corpus, or how many files in the corpus have the word "understand" in them. Similarly, we could ask corpus analysis software to look for lemmatized versions of underst*, such as "understanding," "understood," and "understandable" to display the various forms that this word takes. Of course, this dragnet would also catch words like "understated" or "understudy" should those words also appear in the corpus.

The same kind of question can also be asked about grammatical features. We could ask how often forms of the word "understand" appear as verbs, nouns, or adjectives throughout the corpus, identifying instances when participants might find an "understandable icon" or reference a mental model underpinning their "understanding of what to do." We could also ask more generally about the frequency with which other grammatical objects like conditionals, modals, and conjunctions occur throughout the corpus.

An example of a question of kind comes from David Kaufer et al. (2016), who took a corpus analytic approach to studying citation practices among academics. This work built on research by Andreas Karatsolis (2016) and demonstrated how corpus analytic techniques allow researchers to supplement and guide close textual analysis. The authors asked, "How does the language of citation differ from one discipline to the next and from one level of experience to the next? (Kaufer et al., 2016, p. 462). Their approach was to use DocuScope dictionaries[4] to identify features that vary across the disciplines and vary based on experience (i.e., advisor or advisee). Such distant reading helped identify the features of citation practices that might only become visible when comparing multiple examples.

Another example is Jo Mackiewicz and Isabelle Thompson's (2015) work on writing centers and tutoring strategies, which comes out of corpus analysis of transcribed tutoring sessions and their moment-by-moment interactions between tutors and students. One can get a sense of tutoring sessions by looking at transcripts in isolation, but the authors' computational overview of patterns in those tutoring sessions helps to identify the kinds of moves that tutors make. The authors use corpus analytic techniques to identify words and phrases associated with thought and motivation in order to identify themes like cognitive and motivational scaffolding. This kind of work may be identifiable by asking tutors

---

4.   Phrase lists classified by rhetorical function.

to recall their strategies, but analysis of language use in action is another way to identify regularly occurring discursive work.

Questions of dispersion, following closely upon questions of kind, are those that look at where words or phrases appear in a corpus. In the hypothetical example of a corpus of think aloud protocols, researchers could ask how evenly "understand" or its lemmatized variants are used throughout the corpus or how the use of that term corresponds to particular tasks or if test participants only use the term at particular times during the test. If in answering a question of kind we determine that a word is frequently used, questions of dispersion can let us know whether the word is evenly characteristic of the whole corpus or maybe just indicative of a few files in that corpus.

Peele (2018) offers a good example of a question of dispersion. The article examines the kinds of rhetorical moves used in student writing, particularly among first year students, to understand their nuance and placement in texts. Patterns like objection, concession, and counterargument (p. 83) were tracked to identify how often they occurred and where in a student's papers (i.e., across which rhetorical contexts). The large-scale corpus analysis allowed the author to generate a programmatic understanding of how well student writers were incorporating and employing various rhetorical techniques. This perspective might not otherwise be easy to generate or do so with enough certainty to drive teaching and faculty development strategies (p. 82)

Another example, close to technical communication, could be tracking the dispersion of conditional language in a corpus of instructional discourse. The research question might be how often and where in a corpus writers engage the readers by asking them to consider alternatives or possibilities by using modal language or conditional constructions like "if" or "if you" (e.g., Swarts, 2022) A similar dispersion study is the subject of the example analysis featured in Chapter 6.

Questions of association typically give us information about how often words or phrases appear together, appear in sequence, or fail to appear in sequence when they might be expected to do so. Returning to the running example of a think aloud corpus, we can determine, for example, what words occur together with a word like "understand." Particular functions, interface elements, or user actions may be mentioned at the same time or within close proximity. The collocation (exact or proximal) can give us clues about words that are used together often enough that we should potentially account them as associated. The nature of that association will likely come out of qualitative inspection of the broader context in which the word appears. With the example of "understand," words before might indicate who or what is understanding and words after may indicate who or what is being understood.

Questions of association are of great importance for supporting the more inferential questions that we cover in the coming pages. While the inferential questions attempt to understand what linguistic features might mean in the context of a corpus being studied, these questions must start with observations of associations or the collocation of linguistic features in corpora.

A good example of study addressing a question of association is Joanna Wolfe's (2009) study/critique of technical communication textbooks. The research started from the concern that advice given in technical communication textbooks is *not* associated with conventional writing or citation practices found in professional engineering writing. Additional concerns pertain to the lack of information about data visualization techniques and guidelines regarding writing about data. The question of association that Wolfe addresses in this corpus analysis of 12 technical communication textbooks is clearest when considering characteristics about passive and active voice, as well as citation practices, to determine how prevalent each characteristic is in professional engineering writing and then checks those associations against guidelines offered in the textbooks. Questions that associate advice with actual practice allow us to assess how writing instructions coming through technical communication textbooks might be systematically inconsistent with engineering practice.

A second example comes from Laura Aull and Zak Lancaster (2014). The authors examined the association of linguistic features with the stances that first year student writers take in their texts. The authors' 4,000–text corpus first shows a breakdown of metadiscourse, including hedges, boosters, code glosses, and contrastive connectors used by these writers (a question of kind). The findings show that there are differences between advanced writers and first-year writers in terms of how their stances are associated with different features. Advanced writers are likely to use hedges and reformulation markers that more conventionally demonstrate limited and constrained positions. First year writing students rely more on stances associated with boosting words (e.g., "very" and "certainly") alongside contrastive words. Furthermore, if we consider the main difference between advanced writers and first year writers as being one of time spent acquiring expertise and experience in writing, the differences in stance could be investigated as a question of time: do writers take different argumentative stances as they acquire more experience as writers?

Questions of time are closely related to questions of association but additionally presume that the chronological sequence of words tells us something about the nature of their association. We can read the passage of time into many kinds of discourse. When reviewing spoken discourse, we know that the people who experienced the speech perceived a temporal order to that speech, in that one thing was spoken before something else. Likewise, printed discourse also has a temporal aspect to it. Assuming that content is read linearly, readers experience text temporally as they read it: there is some content that read first and some content that follows, which often makes presumptions about what readers have already encountered. Or, if our corpus is set up to show variation in discourse that happens over time (e.g., collected public speeches or a record of newspaper articles) then analyses can show how words and phrases change over the course

of the time that is built into the corpus. A question like "how does a test participant's 'understanding' of the interface change over the course of the test?" can
tell us something about how that word and its collocates reflect a user's changing
mindset or attitude about a product/interface as the test goes on.

Questions of time are more difficult to come across in the literature of technical communication; although many studies of associational questions have temporal components built in. Aull (2017) provides a good example of how to use
corpus data to answer questions of association that we could reasonably assume
to be time-based. Aull sought to examine how the language use patterns associated with one genre of writing influenced other kinds of writing. This question
of association is time based because of the assumption that exposure to the influential genre of writing must have preceded the writing where we would expect
to see its influences. Aull first developed a "sociocognitive profile" of different
genred forms of writing (p. 4) and then examined how those grammatical and
discursive features appeared in other genres. Although there was no strong statistical support for the influence of argumentative discourse on other kinds of
written discourse, the corpus techniques provided a clear picture of how such
analysis might find systematic associations such as those Aull predicted.

Questions of meaning aim to elicit description of what is going on in a corpus. Following the definition of "aboutness" offered by Mike Scott (1997), these
questions would seek to characterize the content of a corpus. Key words can give
researchers a pretty good awareness of what a body of texts is about. The same
insights can also come from a study of common phrases, especially those that
incorporate use of key words. For example, consider what we might learn looking
at a corpus of figure captions from articles published in a variety of technical
communication academic journals. An analysis of aboutness would tell us both
what those captions are about and, provided that we compared the words of the
journals' captions, something about how those figure captions address readers
differently.

An example of a question of aboutness and meaning is Agboka's research on
localization efforts in pharmaceutical products for distribution in Ghana (2013).
In this study, Agboka collected a small corpus of pharmaceutical documentation
for the Ghanaian market and analyzed how the pharmaceutical products were
discussed. Among the numerous localization problems found was a consistent
lack of specificity and imprecision in the language that might otherwise have
been alleviated, had the documentation been appropriately localized. Consider
how aboutness may help corpora regarding localization. Effective localization
requires awareness of how products are positioned in networks of politics, eco-
nomics, law, and ideology. Documentation that attempts localization needs to
be about those networks and the language used should reflect that aboutness. A
corpus analysis focused on keyword analysis would provide some insights about
whether documentation is effectively localized. It could also be useful in examining effectively localized documentation to see what kinds of aboutness it portrays.

Likewise, take two corpora of scholarship from any field, focused on any topic. An example might be technical communication research on uses of taxonomy in information architecture for digital archives. One corpus might be composed of work by BIPOC scholars and the other of work by non-BIPOC scholars. What would an analysis of keywords and their contexts of use tell us about the differences in what those contributions are about? For example, would they tell us anything about what are considered meaningful taxonomic categories when building a digital archive? This topic is the subject of an ongoing dissertation that Jason is directing. Early results suggests that taxonomic labels like year, domain (e.g., sports, academics, campus life) may miss meaningful categories like communities and events that offer meaningful context.

As we will demonstrate in Chapter 5, some corpus analysis tools allow us to visualize the answers to observational questions. Graphing tools allow us to plot absolute and relative frequencies of words and phrases (questions of kind). Time plots allow us to understand how words or phrases are spread through or grouped in a corpus (questions of dispersion and time). Collocation graphs can show how words and phrases are linked to each other, in what direction, and at what distance (questions of association). Graphs can also show clusters of commonly occurring words that can give clues about what a corpus is about (questions of aboutness) and how those larger themes might be connected as well.

◾ Inference Questions

Inference questions are those that build upon observable patterns of word frequencies and collocations, treating those patterns as evidence of something larger. For example, observing a collocation of variants of the word "understand" near discussion of a group of icons on an interface could be treated as evidence that those icons are a source of interest (either of understanding or lack of understanding). Answering inference questions requires support from frequency and dispersion. Inference questions may also require data sampling that pulls in representative segments of data for coding, using a more traditional qualitative data coding approach (Geisler & Swarts, 2019; Saldaña, 2016).

Questions of identity allow researchers to ask about characteristics of the entire corpus that might help identify its function or significance relative to other corpora. For example, consider the question of style. If we have two corpora that we want to compare because they represent two different stylistic approaches to a task (e.g., instructional content written as topics vs. instructional content written as chapters), we can describe the corpora in terms of their differences in word and phrase frequencies, associations, and temporal sequences. These differences or similarities between corpora can then tell us something about the lexical or grammatical features that constitute characteristic differences in those corpora. For example, a finding that instructional content, written as topics, contains more pointing metadiscourse compared to instructional content written as chapters may reflect a difference in how the content across those formats will be used or what kinds of user actions are supported.

A different way of asking questions of identity about corpora is to examine keywords (see the discussion of keyness in Chapter 2), as questions of meaning allow us to do. We can compare two or more similar corpora and ask what words occur with unusual frequency or which words are unusually absent in a corpus. We can also discover *negative* keywords: words that are unusually absent in one corpus by comparison to another. For example, we could ask questions of identity about a corpus of apology letters from CEOs. If we compare those letters to a corpus of template apology letters, what lexical and grammatical features, what associations, and what sequences of words differentiate CEO apologies from typical business apology letters? What words appear more frequently than in the template apologies, and which words appear less frequently? The answers to these questions, based on the differences uncovered, could say more about what CEOs use apology letters to do that is not assumed in business communication textbooks talking about the purposes of apology letters.

An example of a study taking up a question of identity is Ishizaki's 2016 study of crowdfunding proposals from Kickstarter. The study focused on crowdfunding proposals in the "technology" category. Within this dataset, Ishizaki examined crowdfunding proposals that were successful and compared them with crowd-funding proposals that were unsuccessful. The article identified traits that reliably distinguished the contrasting proposals and that appeared to account for their success (i.e., the inference). The conclusions about appeals to specialized or general audiences provide some information about the characteristics separating successful from unsuccessful proposals.

Anson et al. (2019) offer another good example of a question of identity. Their study attempted to understand the discursive practice of "text recycling" as a common but overlooked writing strategy. The problem of identification was that popular plagiarism-sniffing technology can identify when text is being reused but cannot distinguish between legitimate and illegitimate instances of text reuse (p. 129). Consequently, a bigger collection of examples is needed to fine tune the ability to both identify and distinguish such uses of textual reuse.

One final example of a study asking a question of identity is Dryer's (2013) study of the concept of "writing ability" as it is instantiated in rubrics. This study offers an excellent methodological explanation of corpus-assisted analysis that combines both quantitative and qualitative analysis to portray a familiar, but sometimes fuzzy, concept to scholars of writing. By finding language patterns in grading rubrics, Dryer is able to get some insight about traits and other performance qualities that educators rely on when pointing to and identifying "writing ability."

Questions of use examine the pragmatic ends that are achieved through the use of particular words or phrases in a corpus, that is, how people use words to do things. These kinds of questions build on aboutness (but go beyond what the corpora are about to how the words themselves are used to do things. For example, imagine that we had a corpus of language from user contributions made to a GitHub repository for developing mapping software. We could ask how developers and users contributed to the development of the software. If we were to examine how textual contributions made by users differed from those made by developers, we could interpret those language patterns qualitatively to discover how users and developers settled into roles in the repository that are reflected in the language of their contributions. Furthermore, by examining the substance or success of those contributions, we might gain insight about the most effective kinds of contributions that people tend to make to the repository.

An example in published literature is Cate Cross and Charles Oppenheim (2006), who offer a small-scale corpus analysis of scientific abstracts (12 total) to illustrate how abstracts function. Part of their stated research purpose was to "define the typology and functions of abstracts to fully understand their purpose, scope and use" and to "establish the structure of science abstracts through the definition of 'moves'" (p. 430). The result is an identification of characteristics in science abstracts that move the discussion toward certain rhetorical ends while moving through different domains of content (e.g., participant, discourse, hypothesis, and real-world domains). The study gives readers a better sense of the kind of thing that scientific abstracts are (i.e., question of identity) and the uses to which they are put.

A number of other studies also use corpus techniques to get at questions of use. Arthurs (2018), for example, uses corpus techniques to examine how undergraduates whose essays comprise the Stanford Study of Writing corpus change their use of language, both in terms of syntactic complexity and in their discursive stance toward their arguments (pp. 140–141).

Similarly, Barton (1993) offered an analysis of stance and how experienced writers and inexperienced student writers use evidentials, words expressing an attitude toward the knowledge created. For Barton, the clues that differentiate experienced versus inexperienced use of evidentials are in the linguistic variations, extracted and elaborated with examples to show the rhetorical/grammatical variation in use.

Questions of convention could potentially be related to questions of meaning and use. These questions allow us to interpret meaningful patterns of discursive action that arise around particular work practices. Similar to research that we have seen on genre (e.g., Swales, 1990) and genre-related work practices (e.g., Spinuzzi, 2003), we could draw inferences about emerging forms of discourse that are used to accomplish particular kinds of work or to mean specific things to different communities of practice. For example, if in studying the output (e.g., meeting notes) from different organizational communities of practice, we could look for patterns of lexical and grammatical choices that indicate some kind of deliberate communicative activity or discursive repertoire (e.g., Wenger, 1998) that might be critical to the work that this community does.

Barton (2004) also provides an example of corpus studies used to examine conventions. In a 2004 study, Barton used corpus techniques to describe how physicians used different language and took different stances toward knowledge claims when speaking with patients (i.e., "front stage" interactions) versus talking with colleagues or the researcher (i.e., "back stage" interactions). The differences that show variation in both directness and certainty reveal not just that front and back stage interactions are different but that they do different kinds of work. And the similarities between front stage interactions and back stage interactions offers a vivid picture of the conventions associated with those interactions.

Omizo and Hart-Davidson (2016b) likewise use a corpus approach to studying citation moves made in academic writing. After building a tool to analyze scraped text and determine both the textual characteristics and spatial characteristics (e.g., relative to other claims in a paper) the authors were able to generate findings that could be used to distinguish approaches to citation making that differed by discipline or writer experience.

Thinking through different types of questions will reveal a variety of potential entry points into a corpus, often more than can be feasibly undertaken in a single study. However, this is a good sign—a good corpus will support many studies. The way to decide how to select questions and proceed with analysis is to consider the theoretical framework that will guide the overall analysis.

▌ Using a Theoretical Framework

Most research is undergirded by a theoretical framework that describes who or what is involved with a research phenomenon, the contexts where this research phenomenon exists, and the conditions under which it occurs. The theoretical framework helps researchers understand the relationships between the actors and contexts involved with the phenomenon being investigated. For example, as we will note in Chapter 6, the literature on writing for coherence and cohesion leads to some theories about what kinds of function language and grammatical constructions are related to the creation of coherent and cohesive writing.

Theoretical frameworks can help us determine what lexical or grammatical features to pay attention to in a body of discourse. They can also help us determine how to build our corpora in order to pull together a collection of discourse that allows us to see the phenomenon that a theoretical framework describes. The same theoretical frameworks can also help us determine what kinds of corpora might make for useful contrasts, which can help us pinpoint characteristic and distinctive discourse features.

A theoretical framework also helps with the selection and coding of discourse after we have found patterns of lexical and grammatical association that appear meaningful. The reason we need theory underpinning corpus analysis studies is that the distant reading supported by word and phrase counts will reveal numerical and visual abstractions about the phenomenon under investigation, while the theoretical framework will help us interpret those abstractions.

From this theoretical understanding of our phenomenon, we can develop coding definitions (Saldaña, 2016). Coding definitions allow us to identify discourse features that are observable and countable while still being connected to the theories that underlie them. As we find more of these patterns of discourse and get a measure of their magnitude and dispersion in the corpus, we can more readily interpret quantitative patterns in light of what the theoretical framework leads us to expect.

In situations where theory may not be robust enough to be a guide, we can identify patterns of discourse that lead to analysis and allow theory to emerge. Qualitative researchers can use a comparison of qualitatively coded samples of discourse to *develop* a theory that explains their relationships (Glaser & Strauss, 1967). The same kind of work in corpus analysis can signal theoretical significance through the quantitative patterns of language use in those samples.

For example, research shows how scientists use modalized language and hedging words to present scientific claims (e.g., Fahnestock, 1986; Latour & Woolgar, 1979), but the labor required to investigate such language use at scale is intense. That analytic effort alone might make it difficult, for example, to carry out a large-scale comparison of scientific claims in pre-publication forums compared to published versions of the same research. However, taking the underlying theoretical framework of hedging and modal language, one could develop an expectation of what those modalized claims would look like and then look for those language patterns with corpus analytic software. And so, the theoretical framework might lead to a question of association (e.g., what kinds of modal language are used in pre-publication vs. publication forums?) that builds to a question of identity (e.g., how do writers present their claims in pre-publication vs. publication forums?) all traced through observable, countable patterns of modal language use. The patterns might help differentiate corpora of scientific discourse that we assume to be contrastive (e.g., pre-publication vs. published). If the theoretical model holds, one could use the observed patterns to select samples for close, qualitative analysis. But if the pattern does not hold, one could do more exploratory analysis to find whether the corpora are meaningfully different on any other grounds.

The movement between quantitative and qualitative analysis based on theoretical concerns can also potentially speed the process of analysis and prevent researchers from becoming invested in a qualitative pursuit, only for it not to yield conclusive results.

Answering Questions: Distant and Close Readings

By this point, it may already be apparent that all of the questions elaborated above could feasibly be answered without a corpus, provided that the researcher sampled well from the data sources. Arriving at good answers through a close reading of a limited number of samples depends on choosing samples that truly are representative of the broader discourse from which they are drawn. If they are not, we may still arrive at results, but those results could be too narrowly focused or might misattribute commonality to a pattern that is only accidentally common in the sample taken. A different approach to answering these questions is make a distant analysis of a more comprehensive and representative data set.

Distant reading questions allow the researcher to ask "what," "when," and "how many." Distant reading questions can look like, "what types of words appear next to the target word in this corpus?", or "when does this word appear in a text (beginning, middle, or end)?", or "in this chronological corpus, when is a word more common (early, middle, or late in the corpus)?", or "how many times does Word A appear in comparison to Word B?" These questions can result in numerical data, but this numerical data does not by itself result in knowledge. Results must be placed in the context of literature and of a real-world problem to become knowledge. For example, a corpus of 300 accepted grants from a ten-year span could have a variety of "what," "when," and "how many" questions that look like the ones asked above. However, the counts do not say much on their own. When placed in the context of the question "what does the language of a successful grant look like?", the patterns of language use in a variety of grants could result in knowledge which answers that question. These specific types of questions that corpus analysis is adept at answering can be deployed in the service of larger questions that point toward real-world answers to real-world questions.

In contrast, corpus-assisted close reading invites you to consider the value of switching between two different kinds of analysis: close and distant (Figure 3.1).

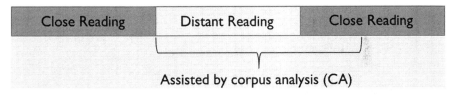

Figure 3.1. The analytic cycle of moving between close to distant to close reading.

Analysis may start with a close reading, finding texts and conversations that give an initial inkling about what might be interesting from a theoretically grounded standpoint. At that initial stage of close reading, we develop intuitions about the texts based on the numerical results. We observe those texts in their contexts. From those contexts, we can develop a sense of how the results may fit with the theoretical framework. Where corpus analysis becomes a boon is when we want to study a broader selection of similar texts in order to identify linguistic patterns that might be easy to overlook upon close inspection of a small selection of texts. In this middle phase of distant reading, the aim is to detect and visualize patterns in the data (Mueller, 2019). We can run analyses that create abstractions for visualizing patterns in data (e.g., word lists, word clouds).

The final close reading phase is when we go from what is learned via distant reading back to the texts. We closely read the texts that best represent the patterns distant reading suggested as germane to the theoretical framework. Distant reading allows us to better sample instances from the corpus that are closest to the phenomenon that we want to discuss.

This combined approach of distant quantitative reading combined with a close qualitative reading might be thought of as computer-assisted close reading. Computer-assisted close reading allows researchers to answer questions that are different from strictly quantitative or qualitative questions. In a grant-writing study, for example, these types of questions could help answer questions such as "what types of arguments are made in the introduction of successful research grants?" To assess this, corpus analysis could assist by identifying unusually frequent terms in the text that would be worthwhile to study further. We could then assess sentences and paragraphs that include those frequent words and qualitatively evaluate what the arguments are. Or, we may examine the patterns of words that appear next to each other with great frequency. These collocations address a question of convention: the conventions across the corpus could reveal types of core ideas that reflect arguments or rhetorical moves in a piece (Swales, 1990), which is otherwise difficult to do. Instead of beginning with the qualitative work of identifying moves, computer-assisted close reading can identify patterns of words that appear across multiple texts in distinctive patterns that suggest what might be studied up close.

▌ Limitations

Although we can and have responded to reservations about corpus analysis, there are still limits to the method. Frankly, corpus analysis is ill-suited to some research situations. Not every problem can be answered with a corpus, as some research questions are better suited to surveys or statistical analysis of relationships. Further, not every type of question has a corpus associated with it: close analysis of eight reports may be better than corpus analysis in a case where eight reports are all that are available or are known to be representative of the broader field of discourse use one wants to talk about. The assumption of size suggests that a corpus needs to be sufficiently large for the benefits of corpus analysis to appear, and some questions simply don't have enough data yet to create a corpus. Even in situations where one can build a corpus, doing so might not be necessary—it all depends on how one achieves representativeness in sampling (consider Chapter 4).

Even with corpora available, there are types of research that corpus analysis can do in only a limited way, if at all. For example, corpus analysis has limited ways to assess tone. Sentiment analysis is the best method currently available, and it is limited in its ability to detect nuance. Neither is corpus analysis always the best choice for studying complex arguments. Move analysis and large-scale dispersion analysis take quite a bit of work on top of distant or close reading to develop. It can be done, but it takes a large amount of effort over a long period of time for results that must be thoroughly hedged. Assessing audience shifts is also a challenge for corpus analysis. Indicator words may help assess some changes in audience, but we would expect that a more global understanding of each document would be needed to make complex arguments about this phenomenon.

Certainly, corpus analysis can be of assistance in research questions like the preceding. For example, semantic analysis that utilizes a probabilistic semantic tagger (http://ucrel.lancs.ac.uk/usas/) can yield key words and phrases that could be tracked via corpus analysis. However, the method is unlikely to be the best standalone solution.

In spite of these limitations, corpus analysis can be a useful tool for gaining perspective on a large data set and using those quantitative findings to shape a closer, qualitative reading. The example studies cited above demonstrate the potential of such a combined approach in writing studies and technical communication alike. In fact, we believe that the most satisfactory answers to questions will come from moving between quantitative analyses of the whole corpora and qualitative analysis of examples that make up those corpora. Because we study language and rhetoric, there is often a need to switch back to the living language to assess what nuance might be yielded. Context for answers from descriptive questions can also be supplied by the literature that gives rise to the questions, although using examples from the corpus further strengthens arguments of this type.

This chapter has been about how to plan a research study of a corpus. Some important issues remain. Chief among those issues is how to build a corpus that can support your analysis plan. As we discuss in the next chapter, building a corpus is more complicated than simply collecting texts. Just as one would not generally interview random people or collect sample texts indiscriminately, neither should one build a corpus without thoughtful attention to what one wants to study.

4. Building a Corpus

This chapter will take a relatively narrow and practical focus on corpus development. Our point is to underscore the importance of developing a strong corpus because research conclusions will only be as representative, balanced, diverse, and valid as the corpus under study. Toward that end, this chapter will focus on what a corpus is and what qualities make a good corpus. We will also discuss how big a corpus should be and how to navigate ethical issues concerning corpus creation. We conclude by discussing some guidelines for cleaning the data that go into the corpus and for annotating that corpus to support analysis.

What is a "Good" Corpus?

One might be tempted to reply to the question by suggesting that bigger is better—a good corpus is a sizable corpus. However, when describing how to decide on the ideal size of a corpus, Randi Reppen (2010) wrote that "for most questions that are pursued by corpus researchers, the question of size is resolved by two factors: representativeness (have I collected enough texts (words) to accurately represent the type of language under investigation?) and practicality (time constraints)" (p. 32). The issue of representativeness requires explanation because determining what counts as representative requires interpretation and ethical discernment. On the other hand, practicality is a relative measure, depending on a researcher's circumstance. There are some techniques of editing and annotating the data in a corpus that can make corpus analysis more practical as well.

Representative

A "good" corpus is one that captures or "represents" the phenomenon that is of interest: "[A] corpus must be 'representative' in order to be appropriately used as the basis for generalizations concerning a language as a whole" (Biber, 1993, p. 243). Douglas Biber goes on to define representativeness as "the extent to which a sample includes the full range of variability in a population" (1993, p. 243). Although Biber is writing about the construction of a corpus that would support analyses and conclusions about language in general, the same consideration applies to more specialized corpora (see Baker, 2006, p. 26).

Analyzing language as a whole would require a representative sample of language on the whole, as massive corpora like the Corpus of Contemporary American English (https://www.english-corpora.org/coca) try to do. Scholars in writing studies, however, generally study more specialized subsets of language. The subsets might be student papers in a technical communication class, white papers from alternative energy companies, position statements from activist groups, tutor/student exchanges in a writing center, or anything else.

Even in those specialized situations, one can strive to collect texts representative of the kinds of language performances that make up that set. In this sense, representativeness, even on a smaller scale, still applies: "a thorough definition of the target population and decisions concerning the method of sampling are prior considerations" (Biber, 1993, p. 243). We just need to be clear about what defines the corpus and the scope of the collection process in order to stay consistent with the phenomenon that the corpus is intended to represent (Atkins et al., 1992).

When sampling texts to include in a representative corpus, Biber encourages us to consider two qualities: "(1) the range of text types in a language, and (2) the range of linguistic distributions in a language" (1993, p. 243). The latter, linguistic domain representativeness, refers to gathering a series of texts that represent the range of linguistic attributes. In technical communication, the range of linguistic variation might simply refer to the range of rhetorical activities that a group engages in (e.g., papers written in a class, genres produced by an NGO, typical conversational moves made in a courtroom). A review of corpus analyses shows that "most researchers associate representativeness with target domain representativeness (i.e., the extent to which a corpus represents 'the range of text types in a language')" (Egbert, 2019, p. 30), but not linguistic representativeness. In truth, we should strive to create corpora that both come from the same target domain and show the range of approaches shown in content from that domain. For example, a representative corpus of business communication from a telecommunications company should include not just different genres of business communication (e.g., reports, email, meeting transcripts, work orders, post-it notes), but also texts from within those genres that use different textual approaches (e.g., formal emails to clients, informal emails to managers, casual emails to colleagues, informational emails to oneself).

To the extent that we know what the range of these text types and linguistic attributes might be, we can choose a sampling strategy that includes as many relevant rhetorical performances as possible from the population under study. Here, "population" refers to the full and total range of language samples from which the corpus could be built. In other words, the more we know about the population we want to study, the better able we are to sample from that population in a way that represents the range of rhetorical performances. Atkins et al. put the matter this way: "[w]hen a corpus is being set up as a sample with the intention that observation of the sample will allow us to make generalizations about language, then the relationship between the sample and the target population is very important" (1992, p. 7) This process goes by different names, such as a "descriptive framework" (Geisler & Swarts, 2019, p. 34) or the "parameters" that include setting, actors, events, and processes that define the activity in a given context (Creswell, 1994, p. 149). A descriptive framework puts on a context in which rhetorical actions are taking place and allows researchers to evaluate the range of data sources that pertain (Gee, 2005; Goffman, 1974; Heritage, 2012):

> "[R]epresentative" means that the study of a corpus (or combination of corpora) can stand proxy for the study of some entire language or variety of a language. It means that anyone carrying out a principled study on a representative corpus (regarded as a sample of a larger population, its textual universe) can extrapolate from the corpus to the whole universe of language use of which the corpus is a representative sample. (Leech, 2007, p. 135)

This goal should drive corpus development. In principle, we could minimally achieve representativeness with a single sample from each text type and rhetorical performance of interest, but Barney Glaser and Anslem Strauss are careful to note that "[s]aturation can never be attained by studying one incident in one group" (1967, p. 62). Instead, multiple samples are needed to build a corpus to support analysis and to support the supposition that the framework/context and its associated parameters have been correctly identified. Size of the sample matters exactly for this reason, because we must find enough samples of what might be relatively rare features of language to be a representative corpus (see Biber et al., 2000, pp. 248–249).

To the extent that we can know the boundaries of the framework or frame that we are attempting to study, we should choose samples that both represent the types of texts produced and the kinds of rhetorical actions that are carried out in those texts.

▮ Further Considerations

In addition to being representative of a language phenomenon, a good corpus will have:

- **Diversity:** Diversity demonstrates language variation across the various places where the language phenomenon is used (Biber et al., 2000). Diverse corpora include a variety of textual sources that attempt to show a wide range of language use from the phenomenon, including prominent and marginalized sources.
- **Balancedness:** having enough samples so that even language phenomena that are relatively rare are included with enough frequency to ascertain variety in their implementation and still be proportionate to the range of text types that make up the corpus in different amounts. The goal is to offer "a manageably small scale model of the linguistic material which the corpus builders wish to study" (Atkins et al., 1992, p. 14).
- **Saturation:** Where to stop collecting samples is an open question. One point of guidance is to follow the iterative procedures of Grounded Theory and attempt to gather enough samples to reach "theoretical saturation," meaning that point when you stop finding examples that expand the range of theoretical criteria that are germane to your study (see Charmaz, 2014; Glaser & Strauss, 1967).

Ultimately, good corpora are those that support valid and reliable research. Validity describes the "ability to measure whatever it is intended to assess" (Lauer & Asher, 1988, p. 140). In corpus analysis, we would expect a valid corpus to represent the rhetorical action or language phenomenon that we wish to study. Effective representation of the rhetorical action would give the corpus "face validity" (Creswell, 1994, p. 121). Face validity, in turn, reassures readers that any analytic query of that corpus has "content validity" or a degree of connection between the theoretical frame represented by the query and the corpus against which the measurement is taken. Reliability is the degree to which measurements or queries will "stay stable over time and among observers" (Krull, 1997, p. 177). A static corpus would tend to support reliable access to the contents and reliable results based on similar queries (Kennedy, 2014). Also, as we work with similar corpora in similar ways and reach similar kinds of conclusions, the overall reliability of those corpora increases (Gablasova et al., 2019). Writing studies research, for example, has built similar corpora of student writing and found compatible results about matters such as citation patterns (Kaufer et al., 2016; Omizo & Hart-Davidson, 2016b), revision strategies (Holcomb & Buell, 2018; Leijen, 2017), and argumentative stance (Arthurs, 2018; Barton, 1993).

Ultimately, we must keep in mind that language and rhetorical acts are living things, meaning that validity and reliability are in tension. Corpora should grow along with the phenomena they represent to increase validity. Yet the result of adding new, contemporary language use to existing corpora is that old analyses based on prior iterations of the corpus may become less reliable. For this reason, reliability is best supported with a well-documented process of corpus creation that can ensure others will build corpora based on the same understanding of the underlying framework.

∎ The Process of Corpus Building

Building a representative corpus is not a simple matter. Even with a plan in mind, the process requires some iteration (Biber, 1993). To Biber, this cycle involves a pilot (an empirical observation of text) leading to theory development, a corpus design plan, corpus sampling to develop a portion of the corpus, and revaluation of the corpus developed to date. Egbert (2019) expands on Biber's cyclical model to include:

1. Establish (and project) research objectives
2. Define the target domain (population)
3. Design the corpus (including sampling frame, sampling unit, sample method, size)
4. Collect the sample
5. Annotate the corpus (relative to your analysis, including metadata about speakers and perhaps parts of speech)

6. Evaluate target domain representativeness
7. Evaluate linguistic representativeness
8. Repeat 3–5, if necessary
9. Report (p. 36)

Although this model assumes that one is attempting to understand general language use, the same process is compatible with more specialized work in writing studies. Taking the author's elaboration of Biber's cyclical steps as a starting point, the process of developing a corpus should start with an understanding of the framework in which the language phenomenon takes place.

Steps 1 and 2 ask us to develop a clear set of objectives for the language phenomenon to be studied, then determine where that language phenomenon is found and who participates in it. Here, all of the lessons about understanding a frame, setting, or descriptive framework are important for determining what the population is. An example could be a study seeking to understand the construction of informed consent for medical and other kinds of research. Because the process of informed consent for a research proposal involves the original content about the study and its risks, templated language from a research office, conversation between a PI and research participant, and perhaps other sources, the researcher seeking to build a corpus would choose which sources of data to include based on the range of participants. The researcher will choose which sources of data to exclude depending on the aim of the research. For example, if we want to understand a particular dynamic of the informed consent process (e.g., PI and participant interactions), we would study texts pertaining to those interactions and not all texts involved in the process of developing, administering, and documenting informed consent.

Step 3 requires determining an appropriate approach for sampling. Although Biber et al. recommend a specific approach for determining representativeness and diversity in sampling for general language use, "sampling techniques from other areas of social sciences can be considered for their applicability to corpus design" (Biber et al., 2000, p. 250). Traditional sampling strategies like typical case, stratified, best case, random, and convenience sampling are appropriate, so long as the presuppositions and limitations of those sampling strategies are taken into account. For example, typical case sampling focuses attention on the most common type of case and loses sight of the range of cases that may appear. A best-case sample artificially selects cases that are most pertinent to the analysis, while overlooking those cases that are not helpful (even if the frequency of unhelpful cases is high). And a convenience sample collects samples without specific regard to their representativeness of the full range of cases that could be included. Each type of sampling has its own positives and negatives to consider.

Practically speaking, however, many corpora will be convenience samples. In some circles, a convenience sample has a pejorative air because it suggests a lack of rigor in approaching the design. However, "convenience" really just means that the sample is not random. Consider the alternative. To get a random sample, researchers would need to know the full size of the population from which to gather a sample, but "most domains of natural language have not been fully indexed and/or are not fully accessible to the compiler" (Egbert, 2019, p. 31). We simply have not indexed the full data set from which to draw a random sample. However, focusing on discrete phenomena can sometimes allow for a comprehensive sample. A technical communicator analyzing a company's documentation from the company's formation in 2000 to the present day may have access to all the documentation in that period. That "sample" is comprehensive, not convenient. If the technical communicator wants to assess a smaller period of documentation, that would be a convenience sample—unless different criteria for comprehensiveness were applied (such as "all documentation addressing Product X, released in 2012").

In Step 4, we collect samples for the corpus, whether piece by piece or comprehensively, using automated means. Piece by piece means that you move copies of files from their original location (wherever that may be) into a corpora that you can use. Automation tools allow software to conduct programmed collection based on rules and criteria. More on these two types of processes below. In Step 5, we add annotations supported by the tools we are using. These annotations might include speaker, location, length, part of speech, or perhaps even some starter codes (see Saldaña, 2016, Section 3). These metadata markers enable a researcher to subdivide a corpus into partitions that might support analysis across a contrast (Lüdeling et al., 2007, p. 10). An example contrast might be expert and non-expert language in a public forum on nuclear energy use in a community.

In Steps 6 and 7, we review the emerging corpus to make sure that it is working toward representativeness. Does the corpus have a range of the kinds of texts that are available in the framework/context that we want to study? Does the corpus include texts that represent the contributions that different participants make? These questions will help ensure domain representativeness. To assess linguistic representativeness, consider what can be learned by analyzing the descriptive framework, frame, or context of the rhetorical activity under study. What kinds of actions and processes do the participants engage in, and how common are those actions and processes? Are there enough samples to look at, even of the rarest actions and processes? Are those samples balanced by having more samples of the more common actions and processes (i.e., balancedness), so as not to over-represent relatively rare actions? For example, in studying a corpus of emergency preparedness documentation, it might be common to identify examples of the imperative mood used to give a command to the reader, using the implied second person. It might be relatively rare, by comparison, to find examples of the first person, representing the author's reflections. But if the first person is used at all, it should be included for representativeness, even if its inclusion is limited to one or two documents.

Step 8 asks us to evaluate the corpus based on the criteria for representativeness and size outlined in Steps 6 and 7, then readjust the corpus design and/or sampling strategy accordingly until the corpus is complete. Then we are ready to report the steps taken to create the corpus in the methods section (Step 9).

■ Corpus Size

We must also consider how capacious a corpus needs to be for the goals of the project to be reached. While collecting a large dataset from a particular website, social media property, or database can be meaningful, the reasons for doing so need to be clearly articulated before, during, and after collection to ensure that the work is not scooping up work that is not necessary for the project.

In general, the more texts we include, the more likely it is for us to amass a corpus that represents the diversity of the rhetorical phenomena that we are interested in studying (Leech, 2007). Understandably, a tendency in corpus development may be to "go big." How can more data hurt the analysis? (Although there is a kernel of truth to the position that *size is good*, there are limits to the usefulness of size. One on hand, we are likely to encounter practical limitations to corpus size. The more data a corpus contains, the harder our poor CPUs have to work to grind through the analysis. Also, more data mean more effort up front to clean and pre-process data for analysis. Finally, gathering types of data that overflow the boundaries of the research plan in an attempt to gain more data may hurt the validity and reliability of the research.

Given that corpora can be too big, corpus analysts have developed several ways of determining the appropriate size of a corpus. Biber (1993) provides precise measures for determining the proper size of a corpus. Even though Biber's focus is on corpora modeling general language use, this approach to determining a size threshold is illuminating. Biber's approach considered a small sample of an existing corpus in order to identify the dispersion of items of linguistic interest. To Biber, the dispersion of nouns, pronouns, verbs, other parts of speech, and tense markers comprised the elements of interest. Biber derived a number of samples to gather based on how often these variables appeared relative to one another and the mathematical threshold for making significant statistical observations. We could take a similar approach.

A more general guideline is a 5:1 ratio of text samples to variables researched. For example, a study of instructional writing looking at 12 different types of metadiscourse markers might want to include a minimum of 60 different text samples (i.e., 5 * 12) as a starting point. However, this guideline assumes an even, random dispersion of the discourse markers of interest and so may not be the best guideline, on its own, for building a corpus of appropriate size.

Even in light of these specific and general guidelines, it is important to remember that approximations for language analysis via corpus analysis are based on assumptions that lead to interpretations about the representativeness of the corpus we develop. For specialized corpora, like the ones we may be interested in developing, we do not need million-word corpora to support the analysis, so long as we make an effort to include enough samples to provide multiple examples of the kind of phenomena we want to study (Baker, 2006). Million-word corpora *could* be used but may not be necessary.

■ Ethics of Corpus Building

As the field of corpus analysis grows and matures, the ethics of building corpora continue to shift and change as well.

■ Internet as Sample Site

The wide-open vistas of the internet and the availability of data scraping utilities have made it easier than ever to find and collect examples of discourse. Given the abundance of textual information that the internet puts at our fingertips, it would seem that search engines make the process of corpus creation easy. With so many websites, forums, and databases full of texts of all types, File>Save seems to be the only technical skill required. In fact, some have argued that robust search engines may even feasibly treat the internet as a corpus on its own (e.g., Fletcher, 2007).

The internet holds further appeal as a source for corpus construction because technical communication scholars and practitioners study many rhetorical activities or language phenomena that are not found or highlighted in venerable, commercial corpora like the Corpus of Contemporary American English (COCA— https://www.english-corpora.org/coca; Figure 4.1), the British National Corpus (https://www.natcorp.ox.ac.uk), or the Brown University Standard Corpus of Present-Day American English (https://www.sketchengine.eu/brown-corpus/). Technical communication practitioners and researchers may need to develop their own corpora because our phenomena of interest belong to genres not covered in commercial corpora or that are too new or specialized to warrant dedicated commercial corpora (Lüdeling, Evert & Baroni, 2007).

Despite the appeal of using the web as a corpus or using web tools like search engines and aggregators to compile corpora for review, the quality of such corpora often cannot be verified. To use the internet as a corpus or a search engine as a tool for corpus construction, we must assume that online search engines surface results that are representative of the dispersion and diversity of rhetorical acts in our studied population. This is a problematic assumption because access to content on the internet is shaped by commercial interests driving search engine algorithms. The assumption is further problematized when considering the differential access that people have to the internet as a platform for recording rhetorical acts. Even if search engines did provide frictionless and representative access to content on the internet, differences in access already may have prevented potential content created outside the internet from appearing on the internet at all.

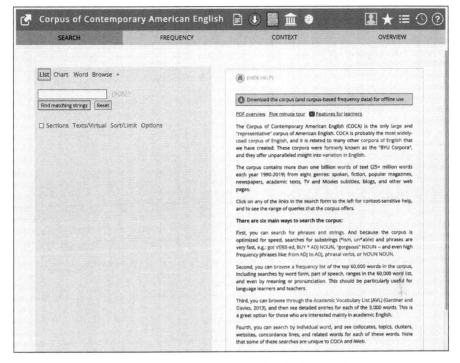

Figure 4.1. Search interface for the Corpus of Contemporary American English (COCA).

Delimiting the population to only that work which is on the internet or on a certain site is a way around this problem, but researchers should always keep in mind that delimiting in this way will exclude the voices of those who could not use the internet to conduct rhetorical actions. The number of offline participants, components, and texts of some contexts are high: political actions, legal actions, judicial actions, civic actions, activism, and education, among them. Situating online findings in the physical, offline context is necessary for projects like these, as well as noting that the online findings represent only one angle on the issue (Degrees of Generalizability in Chapter 2). Consider Ansgar Koene et al. (2015) for a more detailed discussion on this topic.

Access

Finding and accessing representative examples of discourse can prove ethically challenging as well. Access to discourse may require privileged access to communities that could have strong opinions about researchers including their data in a corpus for linguistic analysis, even if they are the intended audience for that research (Baker, 2012). The analyst may be unable to conduct some studies due to the community's decision to shield their data from analysis. This is particularly true of language created in private online or offline communities, where the analyst has access to data but not permission to use it. Even using publicly available data features complex ethics, but the ethics of using private data should include consent of the community or distinctive representatives of the community (if the whole community cannot be reasonably asked to consent, due to size or other conditions).

■ Representation

Given that representatives of private communities can give researchers access and consent to community data, researchers must also be careful about who or what we take to be representative of a particular discourse. If we take a particular kind of discourse to be meaningful enough to study, we ought to examine closely who we take to be the producers of that discourse. Those who we recognize as offering typified examples of discourse are producing what Richard Rorty called "normal discourse" or "that which is conducted within an agreed-upon set of conventions about what counts as a relevant contribution" (1979, p. 320). But not everyone produces "normal discourse," and so selecting discourse examples on the assumption of their representativeness may unknowingly re-instantiate existing power structures (Thralls & Blyler, 1993).

■ Balance

There are ethical issues related to balance as well (Kennedy, 2014). Balance represents a concern with drawing examples from across the range of sources for a particular kind of discourse and determining whether the resulting balance in the corpus gives appropriate or undue weight to any particular source of discourse. For example, insufficient attention to balance could tilt the corpus to favor a dominant power structure. More mundanely, balance also concerns how information from different sources is sampled. If we are dealing with sources of discourse that span different time periods, how and to what extent are those different time periods represented? If various parts of a document are considered separately, is there a balanced presentation of content from the beginning, middle, end, or from the introduction, methods, results, discussion, and conclusion? For example, when studying instructional documentation for the uses of metadiscourse, we would need to consider that a task, a concept, and a reference topic within a documentation set would engage the reading audience differently and, presumably, use different forms of metadiscourse. Sampling for each of these topics, or representing them proportionally in the corpus, should be a consideration.

■ Ethical Guidelines

Building our own corpora in a principled way is necessary in these fraught ethical conditions. The question before us is how to mitigate the ethical risks associated with corpus creation. William Crawford and Eniko Csomay take an approach that imposes restrictions on how the corpus is created and how the results of the analysis might be used:

- Make sure that your corpus is used for private study and research for a class or in some other educational context.
- Research presentation[s] or papers that result from the research should not contain large amounts of text from the corpus. Concordance lines and short language samples (e.g., fewer than 25 words) are preferable over larger stretches of text.
- When compiling a corpus using resources from the World Wide Web, only use texts that are available to the public at no additional cost.
- Make sure that your corpus is not used for any commercial purposes. (2016, p. 76)

This short set of guidelines covers several practical ethical issues. A broader set of ethical principles could guide action across a broader variety of cases. There are reasons why corpora in technical communication may need to be available for corporate use or may need to be made public; for example, corpora that support a broad and distributed research agenda spread across many practitioners or many scholars.

A more nuanced set of considerations comes from the Association of Internet Researchers (AoIR). The authors of the group's 2019 ethical statement on using internet-based data adds a number of other considerations (franzke et al., 2020). Among them is a call for researchers to consider the context in which data is uncovered. By extracting data into a corpus, does the resulting corpus still respect the context in which the sampled content was originally created?

A second consideration is whether there is a meaningful distinction between data and people (franzke et al., 2020). Although a corpus pulls together many examples of discourse from across different speakers/writers, there are still people behind those samples. With improvements in internet searching, it is possible (and increasingly likely) for someone to link passages from corpora back to people who wrote them. Even when following guidelines for appropriate corpus construction, we are still confronted with questions about how we represent human participants whose discourse appears in the corpus.

Researchers must consider the ethics of corpus creation so that the research respects the people whose content is involved and remains valid to the goals of the study. Some researchers may also need to consider the ethics of corpus creation in regard to their institutional context. Corpus creation projects have often been considered exempt projects by Institutional Research Boards in the United States, but this is not always the case. If your IRB or other research ethics oversight in your organization considers corpus analysis projects, you should work with their office to meet the ethical research standards of your institution before sampling your corpus.

Even if your institution does not require official authorization to sample corpora, we recommend thinking through the ethics of the process to appreciate where the discourse has come from and what it represents. These ethical considerations are always situational and can be difficult to resolve. The AoIR ethical statement asks researchers to "foreground the role of judgment and the possibility of multiple, ethically legitimate judgment call—in contrast, that is, with more rule-bound, 'one size fits all' ethical and legal requirements" (franzke, et al., 2020, p. 6). Building a corpus ethically requires a continuous process of evaluating contexts and researcher decisions to ensure that the ensuing corpus is valid, representative, and responsive to local, situational issues surrounding the specific content in it.

■ Ways to Collect Data for a Corpus

Once you have a theoretical framework to guide corpus development; an idea of the size required; a strategy for how to make that corpus representative, balanced, and diverse enough to suit your analytic needs; and an ethical plan for gathering those samples, it is time to make practical decisions about how to collect data.

▌ Piece-by-piece

Part of the challenge of corpus building is the sheer amount of time required to find, download, clean, and save files for analysis. If the files that you have permission to study are found behind firewalls or on secure servers, you may be limited to individual downloads and piece-by-piece cleaning. This old, reliable way to build a corpus, one file at a time, requires saving texts to a folder and then uploading them to a corpus analyzer. Depending on your time and patience, this approach will work fine. This approach often results in developing a better initial awareness of the files in a corpus than when assessing corpora made with automated collection.

▌ Automated Corpus Building

Automated ways of building corpora can remove some of the drudgery of assembling corpora piece-by-piece while also helping make careful corpus building choices.

If your data exists on the open internet in publicly accessible places, a tool like an automated corpus builder could be of use. Although each corpus builder will work differently, they are based on search terms fed to the system and used to search the internet to find sources that are likely to be relevant to your interests. BootCaT (https://bootcat.dipintra.it; consider Figure 4.2) is an example of a tool that uses search engines to run a query against websites and files to come up with a corpus that matches your search terms (see Baroni & Bernardini, 2004; Zanchetta et al., 2011).

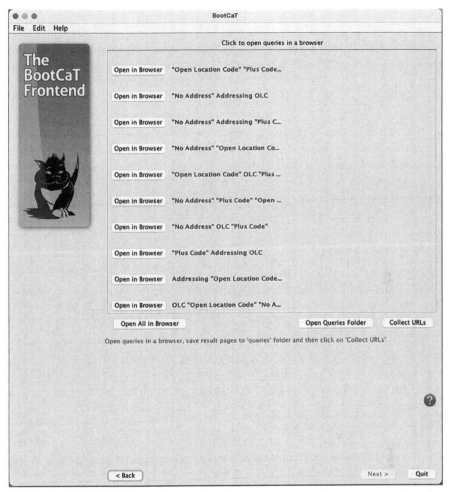

Figure 4.2. BootCaT data collection interface showing "tuple" searching on the web.

BootCaT works by building "tuples," or three-word combinations of search terms, to find more relevant search results (e.g., report technical editing, editing student technical, editing report student, etc.). You have the option to select a search engine, add or exclude domains to search, add or exclude document types, and other settings. After generating the tuples, the system processes custom searches that can be pasted into a search engine. For each set of search results, you copy the URL of the search results and put that set of URLs into a different window on BootCaT. Once all of the search URLs have been entered, BootCaT visits the results, eliminates duplicates, and copies the pages/documents that are indicated. Download the results and you have a corpus. BootCaT documentation suggests that the platform can create a corpus of "typically of about 80 texts, with default parameters and no manual quality checks[,] in less than half an hour" (BootCaT, 2019).

Another set of tools are linguistic search engines, which are emerging technologies that aim to use the "web as corpus." More specifically, these tools use search engines to run a query on all of the sites that it crawls and return findings, like keywords in context, relative to a search term that you have given it (see Fletcher, 2007). An example of such a tool is "KWiCFinder" (https://www.kwicfinder.com/KWiCFinder.html) which formerly allowed users to run queries against the web. Such an approach may be interesting to those seeking to study naturally occurring language and broader language patterns across different contexts of use. However, it seems worthwhile to repeat that search engines are designed to prioritize some web content over others, so one should not trust that the results coming back from a linguistic search are unbiased or as diverse as might be achieved by cultivating a corpus more deliberately. Other tools for corpus building can be researched at https://corpus-analysis.com/ (Berberich & Kleiber, 2023).

▮ Web Scraping

Web scraping has been a prominent tool in developing corpora. Scraping websites requires writing a program that accesses web pages, downloads content from designated content fields, then moves to the next page. Depending on the complexity of the website you want to scrape, this program can be fairly easy to write or very complex. Those without prior coding experience most likely will need to partner with someone who has coding experience to quickly scrape content from the web in an automated fashion or find an open-source scraper that is tailored to the particular platform that you want to scrape. Scraping can be a useful tool in situations where piece-by-piece assembly is infeasible and automated corpus builders offer too small of a set.

However, there are legal and ethical complexities to scraping. Sites that outlaw scraping in their terms of service are a particularly thorny issue. While one American court ruling states strongly that scraping public data from the web is not illegal (hiQ Labs, Inc. v. LinkedIn, 2019), the legality of scraping content from websites that outlaw the practice in their terms of service continues to be debated. Any scraping of data from a platform that states they do not want to be scraped is (at the time of writing) in a legal gray area. Further complicating the issue is that some websites allow certain types of scraping tools and processes (such as the process called "spidering") but disallow other types. The safest thing to do is read the terms of service of websites you would like to scrape, and not scrape websites that do not want to be scraped. However, there can be meaningful reasons that a researcher may choose to ignore these rules and hold to existing court cases as their guide, especially where critique is concerned.

▮ Cleaning Corpus Data

After selecting texts for a corpus and taking steps to get those files stored and assembled in a readable format, we should take time to consider preparatory steps that will make analysis easier. The first preparatory step is cleaning the data. Cleaning data consists of removing three types of data: extraneous or anomalous technical information, data specifically required to be excluded from the analysis, and data that are not intended for the analysis.

▋ Extraneous or Anomalous Technical Information

Extraneous or anomalous technical information often appears as a byproduct of the corpus creation processes (scraping, downloading, saving, file transmission, or a combination of these). Junk characters may be generated when scraped files are converted into human-readable formats. These junk characters can take the form of fully or partially garbled records (e.g., andsodxuewrghxf Thefhtrgyoo-iuhshurgqw United Standdgti nxdyer), non-content-bearing characters (e.g., ¡•§¡•§¡•§, ¡•ª¡¶ªᵒ, ∞∞, ªᵒ), numbers appended to a full record (e.g., The European Union.26589720921307561589737324862434), or other types of alphanumeric noise in the corpus. This anomalous information should be removed from the corpus to the extent possible. Although each of these noisy pieces of text will likely be unique and thus not interfere with the process of finding textual trends, they do represent extra work that corpus tools will have to do, as well as potentially broken results to be discovered and discarded later.

"Special characters" that fail to translate in the process of scraping should also be cleaned. Special characters such as ñ or ö may have been turned into a short string of characters in the process of turning the scrape into readable data. Unlike the previous type of anomaly, this form of broken text will often reappear in the same form repeatedly, as tools often transliterate special characters into the same characters each time the special character appears. This type of error might look like this: âeœcatalyzingâe, Smithâe™s, or rÃ©sumÃ©. (These three results should be "catalyzing," "Smith's," and "résumé," respectively.) Given the potential recurrence of this type of error, find and replace can be particularly helpful here.

If the analysis tool supports the special characters that the scrape has broken, then the errors should be corrected. If the tool does not support certain special characters, it is best to replace them with an approximation (e.g., n instead of ñ) instead of leaving the broken characters in the middle of a word. To appropriately report findings, the correct special characters should be reinstituted when writing up the results.

File metadata (i.e., HTML, XML) attached to texts in their home environments (e.g., on a website or in a content management system) is also potentially extraneous and unrelated to the content of the texts studied. Removing these extraneous types of data are often part of the process of developing a corpus. Deleting these types of content from the corpus requires only a note that the researcher deleted junk characters; delineating the type of junk characters is a very high level of detail that would be unnecessary in all but the most rigorous of research spaces.

▌ Data Required to Be Excluded

The second type of information to be eliminated is anything specifically excluded from analysis. For instance, a company may decide to pursue edits to their documentation to remove passive voice after editors found several sections of documentation that could have been more effective in active voice. These editors edited the sections of the text into active voice to demonstrate how this edit is effective. Doing a corpus analysis of all documentation to determine how often passive voice is used and to identify areas of need might exclude those pieces of documentation that have already been edited explicitly to remove passive voice. Including them in the analysis would overrepresent active voice because the sections of documentation have already been adjusted from their original state.

Depending on the audience for the final analysis, material that is sensitive, proprietary, or otherwise flagged as not shareable can and should be eliminated from the corpus. This concern may not be relevant if internal data is being shared to internal audiences. However, even a large corpus size may not be enough to obfuscate sensitive information if internal data is being shared with external audiences. This is particularly true if analysis and reporting strategies include quotes from the data as support for the quantitative analysis, as is often the case. Sensitive material, then, should be removed before analysis. Sensitive data is another reason that an analyst may not be able to undertake every corpus analysis project the analyst desires.

The people who created and are included in the texts may also inform decision making about data inclusion. If texts by or about those who are pregnant, incarcerated, minor, or in a similarly protected group are included in the data but are not the focal point of the study, consider omitting the data to minimize unintentional harm to any member of those groups. If a study directly concerns data by or about people in protected groups, consider taking steps to protect these people's texts. Talking with people in the group(s) being researched to assess how individuals may want their texts reported about is a good starting place, while keeping in mind that no one person can represent a whole group's opinions or concerns. Furthermore, researchers might consider summaries or paraphrases of comments instead of direct quotation to avoid publishing traceable segments of text. Even with these processes in place, reporting on texts carries some possibility of traceability and potential risk for those who created texts. (Sometimes that risk may be too high to conduct a study.)

Whether practitioner or academic research, these types of elimination should be noted in the process of writing up results, stated with a short explanation for why the researcher eliminated data.

▌ Data Not Intended for Analysis

The third type of data to clean from a corpus is data not intended for inclusion in an analysis. While the previous two sections list data removed from the corpus for technical and practical reasons, this type of removal is done for theoretical reasons. Good reasons for eliminating data may be that you want to focus on a particular amount of time for the analysis (thus eliminating content from before or after the analysis window), a specific set of documents about a topic relevant to your research question from a larger set of documents (e.g., "reports on power plant emissions from a larger set of all EPA reports"), or a specific set of data that has outwardly identifiable characteristics (e.g., all tweets from the executive committee members of a single organization out of a database of all organization members' tweets).

Any type of data removal outside of the two classes above must be supported with concrete reasons for the removal. This section of the cleaning process can be one of the most difficult and fraught parts of developing a corpus. Leaving too much data in the corpus can result in a lack of results due to a high noise-to-signal ratio. Taking too much out can result in cherry-picking data to fit a goal. Developing concrete, theoretically-grounded reasons for removal of data is essential in this effort. Previous and similar studies' reasoning for inclusion and exclusion can often be of value in determining best practices. Reporting removals of text for theoretical reasons is necessary in your final deliverable.

■ Corpus Annotation

Corpus annotation is "the practice of adding interpretive, linguistic information to an electronic corpus of spoken and/or written language data" (Leech, 2013, p. 2). As the definition suggests, the process is akin to interpretation. Some corpus analysts might argue that adding any kind of interpretation to a "raw" corpus ahead of time is presumptive. We feel that such preliminary analyses should proceed from the files as the researcher collects and cleans them. Annotations created during analysis function in a similar way to the methods of grounded theory, which allow for the development of theory through the process of analysis (see Glaser & Strauss, 1967). Despite its contested status, corpus annotation is a relatively common practice. Different kinds of annotation exist that can be more or less interpretive.

In general, the common choices one has for annotation are representational and interpretive. Within these categories, the kinds of annotations used by corpus linguists get fairly specialized. Yet by looking at some common kinds of annotations, we can get a picture of why corpus annotation might aid your analysis.

▮ Representational Annotations

Representational Annotations are merely descriptive of the various features of the texts included in the corpus, from small linguistic units to page-level and genre-level characteristics. Among the kinds of representational annotations that one can use are (from Leech, 2007, p. 12):

- Orthographic
- Phonetic/Phonemic
- Part of speech
- Syntactic

Orthographic annotation is the separation of a corpus into words or tokens. Often the corpus analysis software will accomplish orthographic annotation automatically and give a summary of the number of words or tokens in the corpus. The same annotation process can also yield a count of the lemmas in a corpus.

Phonetic/phonemic annotation may be less distinctly useful if your analytic interests are at the level of discourse, but they may be of value to linguistic and pronunciation-based analyses. Phonetic/phonemic annotations indicate how a word is pronounced. When studying sociolinguistic phenomena, for example, such annotations might give information that is important for building an analytic contrast.

Part of speech (or POS) annotation is immensely beneficial for many kinds of analysis. As the name implies, texts in a corpus can be annotated to show what part of speech each word represents. Although there are many common "treebanks" used for identifying different parts of speech, a common one is the Penn Treebank (https://www.sketchengine.eu/penn-treebank-tagset/).

Increasingly, corpus analysis tools are capable of processing texts automatically and assigning POS data that is around 97 percent accurate for English language texts (Kuebler & Zinsmeister, 2015). POS annotation can be a significant boon for researchers interested in studying functional properties of language (Pennebaker, 2011) like referential language (e.g., "this," "that," "those," "these") or modality (e.g., "may," "might," "can," "could," etc.). For example, a corpus study looking at decision making in transcripts from design meetings might want to assess how different collaboration technologies facilitate collaborative thinking and decision justification. To get at such claims directly, POS tagging could allow a researcher to focus on person pronouns (tag: PRP) to identify places in the dialogue when such identifiers are used.

Syntactic annotation refers to the process of identifying small syntactic units of information, like phrase types (e.g., nominals, verbals). To our knowledge, there are no tools that support the automated tagging of syntactic units; although, there are tools like DocuScope (https://vep.cs.wisc.edu/ubiq/) that have built in dictionaries that categorize phrases by their rhetorical function and can be used for matching strings of data larger than a single word (see Wetzel et al., 2021). The labor involved in annotating an entire corpus with syntactic information might be so laborious as to make this an impractical step for close analysis of sample texts. Nonetheless, a dedicated team of annotators with a reliable grammar text can make such annotations. Syntactic tagging would be especially helpful for labeling groupings of words by their syntactic function.

In addition to these representational annotations, there are a number of annotation styles that we could describe as more "structural," referring to observable features of a text. Structural annotations might be used to divide corpus texts into units of analysis. For example, if you have a corpus of interviews, you may want to include structural annotations to demarcate the boundaries between contributions to the interview (e.g., question, response). Or you might want to differentiate among structural elements like captions, headings, and footnotes. Because structural elements often (but not always) have discrete, fairly well understood definitions, they can be readily applied.

Interpretive Annotations

Interpretive annotations add understanding to a text in a corpus. You may think of these annotations as codes, in a way. They can range from simple clarifications (e.g., substituting the antecedent noun for a pronoun) or they can move into more subjective and interpretive grounds. Among the kinds of more interpretive annotations are (from Leech, 2007, p. 12):

- Prosodic
- Semantic
- Discoursal
- Pragmatic

It is with these interpretive annotations that we step closer to the annotations readers might be accustomed to using in qualitative analysis. Unlike representational annotations, interpretive annotations are more subjective. As a result, many of these annotation passes require hands-on attention from researchers, which makes them relatively infeasible to apply uniformly to sizable corpora.

As with phonetic/phonemic annotation, prosodic annotation may be more of a niche annotation for some. When annotating prosodic features of language, you are adding information about tone, volume, rising and falling intonation, and other qualities of spoken speech that might get lost in some forms of transcription. This can matter greatly for corpora of languages that rely on tone and inflection for meaning, such as many forms of Chinese, Thai, Punjabi, and Navajo.

Semantic annotation is "concerned with the literal meaning of language" (Kuebler & Zinsmeister, 2015, p. 83). Annotations intended to clarify semantic properties can range from the clarification of ambiguous referents to the identification of specialized words and phrases. Semantic annotation may involve assigning words to specific "semantic fields," which is a domain of meaning (e.g., arts and crafts, emotions, education, time) to which the words belong. For example, one might annotate transcripts of think aloud protocols to designate which domain a user comments refers to (e.g., interface, task, system response, etc.)

To some degree, semantic annotation can be automated with the help of semantic analysis taggers (e.g., USAS: http://ucrel-api.lancaster.ac.uk/usas/tag

ger.html; Rayson, n.d.). Consider Figure 4.3. Semantic annotation also entails the creation of words with lexical affinities, such as synonyms and antonyms. These lexical sets can be constructed fairly reliably, but there is a degree of interpretation required (see Wilson & Thomas, 2013, p. 54).

Discoursal annotations offer more room for interpretation. In general, discoursal annotations look at identifying the relationships between pieces of content in a text. One common use of this kind of discoursal annotation is in functional grammar, where a person may want to annotate a text to identify theme and rheme in a sentence. The theme is the structure or orientational information in a sentence, and the rheme is the remainder of the message that develops the theme (e.g., In matters of technical writing [theme], clarity is paramount [rheme]) (see Halliday, 2004, pp. 64–65).

Another use of discoursal annotations is to improve cohesiveness in a text by noting references between pieces of the text. Discoursal annotation can be used to identify references, allusions, substitutions, metatextual relations, and direct/indirect references between passages in a text (see Garside, Fligelstone & Botley, 2013, p. 71). These kinds of annotations can show relationships between passages that may help identify how, for example, arguments develop over the course of a text. To take an earlier example, a corpus study of building informed consent in medical and other kinds of research might classify and annotate the types of statements and interactions made prior to a research participant reaching the conclusion that they are giving informed consent when agreeing to participating in a study.

Discourse annotations, more than other kinds, seem most like codes in a qualitative analytic scheme. Sandra Kuebler and Heike Zinsmeister offer "four major classes of relations: temporal, contingency, comparison, and expansion" (2015, p. 142), which describe base relationships between discourse units. This list of base types is expandable (p. 151).

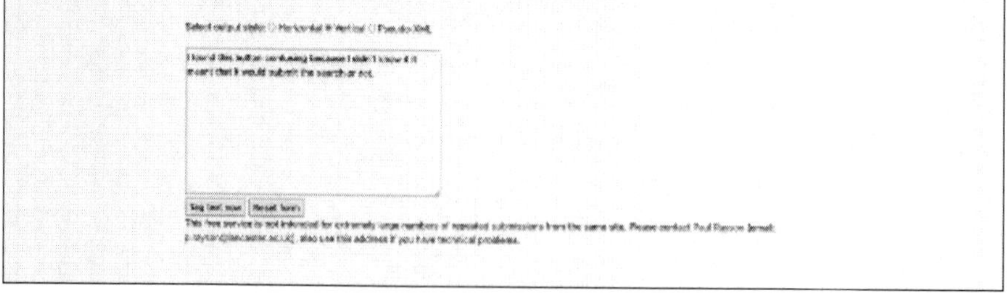

Figure 4.3. Input screen for USAS semantic tagger.

Finally, pragmatic annotations offer information about how we use language, as in speech acts (Leech et al., 2013, p. 91). They are also references to genres, discourses, and styles (e.g., reporting, thought; p. 95). These are known as pragmatic annotations because pragmatics is an examination of "the meaning of language in use" (Kuebler & Zinsmeister, 2015, p. 117). Like discourse annotations, pragmatic annotations closely resemble qualitative analysis codes because they attempt to classify what amounts to speech acts, or routine ways of doing things with words (see Austin, 1962; Searle, 1985).

Pragmatic annotations might also be extendible to show genre characteristics as routine ways that we do things with words in texts. For example, if your corpus consists of reports, you might differentiate report sections (e.g., introduction, methods, results). Sometimes these genre units can have fuzzy boundaries, which makes the application of pragmatic annotations something between structural and interpretive. The annotations may also include those that are much more deliberately interpretive, such as those applied to a discussion where you attempt to annotate the relationship between the responses (e.g., Claim B REFUTES Claim A).

Annotation Processes

There is no correct way to go about annotation or even to decide whether to do it. Each of the above annotation schemes has a variety of protocols and approaches for implementation. A few good practices will help you apply and use annotations well:

- Make sure the annotations can be separated from the raw corpus. Not everyone agrees that annotations should be used when analyzing a corpus.
- Provide detailed documentation about the annotations that you used.
- Try to use annotations that are common among other researchers; previous studies and textbooks can help with this knowledge.
- Symbology (e.g., abbreviations and special characters) should be brief but intuitive to those who would read it.

As for implementing annotation tags in a corpus, many corpus analysis tools support some kind of markup that could be used for adding information to a data set. Some of the most basic markup includes tagsets based on SGML, but customizable ones based on XML are also possible. Tagging often requires using demarcation symbols like <>. These kinds of symbols are important when developing a strategy for understanding what you have annotated, known as a "parsing scheme." Above all, be consistent with the way that you implement annotation, whether you use a convention like an underscore to denote part of speech (e.g., _NN), square brackets to indicate discourse relationships (e.g., [REF Para 2]), or wrapping angle brackets to identify pieces of discourse (e.g., <given> and <new>, as in this sentence: <given> The dry ingredients </given> <new> should be combined with the wet ingredients </new>).

Ultimately, annotations can aid analysis by allowing you to capture intuitions about the data or to apply theory to corpus, creating regular units of segmentation in the data to track the dispersion of language features over the corpus, and/or facilitating the transition from distant readings of a corpus to the close reading. Representational and interpretive annotations can work together (Leech, 2007), because both kinds of annotations add value to a corpus by making systematic and reliable interpretations possible. However, keep in mind that representational annotations may be very limited descriptions of segments of text that can be coded according to a coding scheme, while interpretative annotations require the analyst to do more analytical work to apply an annotation. Also remember that annotation is a kind of manipulation of the data. The details regarding your annotation practices need to be included in a discussion of the methods.

Once you have collected, cleaned, and (optionally) annotated your corpus, the next step is to analyze the contents. Of course, analyzing the content is not nearly as simple as it sounds, if only because of the intimidatingly large amount of data facing you. The way that you may use corpus analysis tools to support analysis that moves from distant to close reading is the subject of the next chapter.

5. Analyzing a Corpus

In Chapter 3, we wrote about the kinds of questions that can be asked of a corpus, ranging from those that track patterns across isolated texts to those that offer a picture of the corpus as a whole. We also discussed the importance of articulating a theoretical framework to guide how we answer those questions. Chapter 4 then detailed how to develop a corpus in which to carry out an analysis. Following the advice in those two chapters, you may now be faced with a corpus of your own, which can be daunting. Although you may know what you want to ask of a corpus, it may not be clear how to employ common corpus analytic tools to answer those questions. The aim of this chapter is to help you think about how to employ tools of corpus analysis to carry out your analysis.

This chapter begins with a description of common types of corpus analysis tools and the kinds of analyses they support. We will draw screen captures from Lancsbox (Brezina et al., 2020) and AntConc (Anthony, 2020), both of which are freely distributed and compatible with multiple operating systems. These tools support approaches that allow comparison across corpora (e.g., to answer questions about identity), comparison between files within a corpus (e.g., to answer questions about time), and within-file comparisons by parsing and structuring files into segmented units (e.g., for questions of use).

In general, these tools support assisted inductive approaches and assisted deductive approaches to answering research questions. Broadly speaking, assisted inductive approaches explore data and build up to theory by working through systematic observations of text. Assisted deductive approaches test out a theory and approach the analysis of text in a top-down way.

Using Functions of Corpus Analysis

Corpus analysis can be an enormous undertaking. Querying a corpus of data that can easily be millions of tokens, in size in a way that supports systematic, critical, and/or comparative analysis can be a challenge. Work at this scale is quite difficult without some sort of machine assistance. Fortunately, there are many good options for tools that support researchers doing corpus analytic work. Among the more effective tools are those designed by corpus linguistics researchers. These tools are designed to have functionality that supports the most common kinds of descriptive and comparative analyses. After reviewing two tools, AntConc and Lancsbox, we will spend time discussing how functions that are common to both (as well as some that are unique to Lancsbox) are useful for analyzing corpora. Both software projects are being actively developed, so there may be some changes in functionality from the time that we have written this review and when you are reading it.

Developed by Laurence Anthony, AntConc is a corpus analysis and text concordance tool that supports many ways of visualizing patterns in a corpus and performing preliminary analysis (Anthony, 2020). AntConc supports the following:

- **Word List**: creates a list of words that are sorted by frequency. The word list can be modified with a stop list that removes words you have chosen to exclude from analysis.
- **Keyword List**: identifies which words in a corpus under study are "key" (or important to understanding the character of the corpus) by comparing words from the study corpus against a reference corpus (Chapter 2). The analysis can differentiate positive keywords (i.e., words appearing more often than expected in the study corpus) and negative keywords (i.e., words appearing less often than expected in the study corpus).
- **Concordance**: shows all instances of a searched term or phrase in the context where that word or phrase appears (Figure 5.1). This feature can support analysis of word variation throughout a corpus. The **Concordance Plot** tool helps visualize the spread or dispersion of that word or phrase throughout the corpus.
- **Collocates**: displays words that are adjacent (i.e., co-located) to the words or phrases you might search. The function shows the context of those words or phrases but also gives a sense of frequency (Chapter 2).
- **Clusters/N-Grams**: shows the phrases that a word or words appears in. The cluster function supports analysis that changes the size of the phrase or cluster, allowing you to visualize the complex constructions that a word of interest might belong to. The N-gram function supports a similar analysis but looks for all clusters of words above a certain threshold (i.e., 3–grams, 4–grams . . . N-grams).

Another robust tool is Lancsbox (Brezina et al., 2020), which was developed by corpus linguists at the University of Lancaster. Like AntConc, this tool supports most of the common corpus analysis functions, including word lists, keyword analysis, and n-gram/cluster analysis. In addition, Lancsbox incorporates support for:

- **Key Word in Context (KWIC)**: shows which files in the corpus use a search term and includes the context for that word (to the left and to the right), supporting analysis of how use of the term varies. Robust filtering allows one to build more complex search terms and filters (e.g., "if" plus "then" in the first word position to the right).
- **Whelk**: examines the frequency and dispersion of a word throughout a corpus. While a frequency analysis might show that a word is used very often in a corpus, a whelk analysis will reveal how many files use that word and how well distributed the word is in the corpus (Figure 5.2).

Figure 5.1. Concordance tool view of a business letter corpus in AntConc.

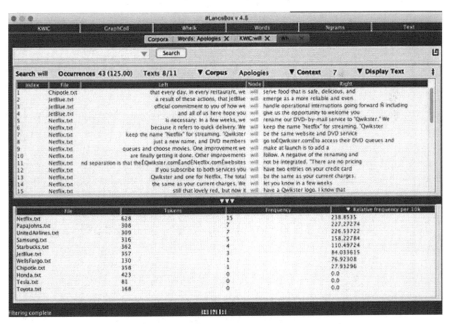

Figure 5.2. Output from the Whelk tool in Lancsbox, showing frequency and dispersion of a search term in a business letter corpus.

- **Graph Collocation (GraphColl)**: visualizes terms that are co-located (i.e., collocates) with the search term of interest. The resulting visualization (Figure 5.3) shows both the universe of collocates in the corpus but also the average distance between the collocate and the search term (e.g., length of line) and the frequency of the collocate pairs (e.g., the density of the line).

Across all of its functions, Lancsbox supports searching by words or parts of speech. Parts of speech are automatically and probabilistically detected by Lancsbox and marked using the Penn Treebank Part of Speech tagset (https://www.sketchengine.eu/penn-treebank-tagset/). In addition, Lancsbox supports a range of sophisticated descriptive and inferential statistics that link directly from the outputs in the software. The Lancaster Stats Toolbox Online (http://corpora.lancs.ac.uk/stats/toolbox.php) offers public access.

AntConc and Lancsbox are just two examples of corpus analysis products that work across different operating systems. Other tools, such as the Windows-based WordSmith (https://lexically.net/wordsmith/), web-based Cortext Manager (https://www.cortext.net/projects/cortext-manager/), and web-based Word-Cruncher (https://wordcruncher.com/docs/) support identical or very similar kinds of corpus analysis. Another tool that we have mentioned previously is DocuScope (public access via https://vep.cs.wisc.edu/ubiq/), which supports phrase-level classification of rhetorical functions.

Try out the tools and learn from experience. Before long, you will understand what kinds of analyses are supported. However, we can offer an overview of how some of the more common functions across Lancsbox and AntConc that have specific application for the kinds of research discussed in this volume.

▌ Word and Keyword Analysis

Using a word or word list function, it is possible to examine word frequencies and dispersions in your corpus. The simplest searches will show you both the absolute (raw count) and relative frequency (percentage proportion of the corpus represented by a word), which can give an immediate look at how common or uncommon a word might be. If you have a reference corpus for comparison, the frequency data can tell you how similar or different the corpora are on a given set of words.

Some tools, Lancsbox being one, will also supply information about how well dispersed a word is throughout the corpus. Dispersion is a measure of spread, and it will give you an idea of where the word appears in the corpus and how commonly. A dispersion rating ranges from zero, meaning even dispersion, to larger numbers that indicate increasingly uneven dispersion. The more even the dispersion the more likely it is that the word being tracked appears in multiple texts within the corpus. Higher numbers may mean that a word appears in just a handful of texts and so might not be indicative of the corpus.

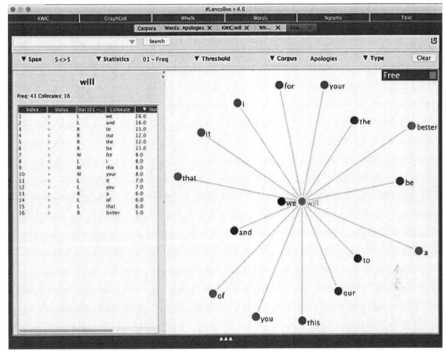

Figure 5.3. Output from the GraphColl tool in Lancsbox, showing the network of collocations for the word "will" in a business letter corpus. The network shows distance (length) and frequency (weight).

You can identify keywords by noting those that are frequently used and well dispersed. For example, imagine a corpus of meeting transcripts from teams using different methodologies for collaboration. As researchers, we might expect there to be differences in the amount and frequency of collaboration in those meetings. A word-based analysis might lead to focusing on proposing words like "how [about]" or "[what do you] think" or "what [about]." A frequency analysis could show whether teams focused on one kind of collaboration methodology use more or fewer proposal words. Likewise, a dispersion analysis could reveal whether the incidence of proposal words is even across groups and whether there are specific places in the meetings where proposals words are more likely to be used.

Through word analysis, it is possible to form a sense of a corpus' "aboutness" or meaning. Although the word search tool enables quick, intuitive searches of word dispersions in a corpus, sometimes our questions aim to get at the meaning of texts in a corpus. In these instances, using a built-in keyword analysis tool can show, on the basis of their mathematical probability of occurring, whether certain words give an indication about what the texts in a corpus mean. When comparing a study corpus to a reference corpus, the software can determine the presence of positive keywords (those appearing unusual frequency), negative keywords (those that are unusually absent by comparison) and sometimes lockwords (i.e., words that appear to be important to the meaning of both corpora).

Assume that it is possible to divide the transcripts from our sample corpus on collaboration into contrastive sub-corpora (e.g., groups using methodology one, groups using methodology two, etc.). Those corpora could then be compared to identify keywords differentiating the groups. Suppose further that a keyword analysis showed that groups using collaboration methodology two used "think" more often than would be expected (i.e., it is a positive keyword) and "should" less often than would be expected (i.e., it is a negative keyword). Such a finding would provide evidence that the kinds of actions going on in one group differ in terms of how proposals are made or suggested.

▪ Keyword in Context (KWIC) or Concordance Analysis

The keyword in context (KWIC) analysis (also known as concordance analysis) is one of the most helpful tools for looking at the location of terms of interest within texts in a corpus. The KWIC tool allows us to get back to the texts from which word and keyword lists are built. These results are called concordance lines (Figure 5.1), and they show all instances where a given word appears across the files in the corpus.

In many KWIC analyses you can set the context size for a given search. In Lancsbox, the default is to provide seven words to the right and left of a search term. However, you might find that it is beneficial to set a deep context (e.g., 20 words to the right and left of the search term) in order to see more of the context to determine how a term is used. Setting a deeper context may also facilitate additional qualitative coding once the KWIC results are downloaded into a CSV file.

An additional advantage of the KWIC analysis is that you get to see more of the variation with which a key term is used. You might find more variations on use than your theory would lead you to expect. You might find uses that do not fit the theory but that seem intriguing nonetheless. Both of these outcomes could then be the start of a new or revised theory.

Or, returning to our sample corpus of transcripts from collaboration meetings, we might decide to interpret the content from a particular theoretical construct. For example, suppose that one aim of investigating group collaboration was to identify whether groups that met only in person, only online, or using a hybrid mix of face to face and online thought of themselves as "communities of practice" (Wenger, 1998). We might look at a list of proposal words generated from a word-level analysis (e.g., "think," "consider," "what [if]," "how [about]") and then examine those words in context, using a KWIC analysis to assess whether those proposal words are used to create "mutual engagement" (shared focus), "joint enterprise" (shared sense of purpose and aims) or a "shared repertoire" (shared means, conventions, resources) (Wenger, 1998, pp. 73–78). The KWIC analysis could show what work the proposal words are doing and support development of a coding scheme to track those functions more precisely.

N-Gram and Cluster Analysis

N-gram analysis allows you to review common phrases in a corpus. The "N" in "n-gram" is simply a placeholder indicating a number. You may search for 3–grams (three-word phrases), 4–grams, 5–grams, etc. Running the N-gram analysis on its own will give a different kind of context analysis. Instead of showing individual words and their contexts within the corpus, N-grams will show the most common phrases appearing across the texts in the corpus. These common phrases may indicate the kinds of rhetorical acts occurring in a corpus. For example, a 3–gram analysis of product documentation might show that phrases where "you" is addressed and is addressed with a conditional "if" indicating a hypothetical context, are common (Figure 5.4).

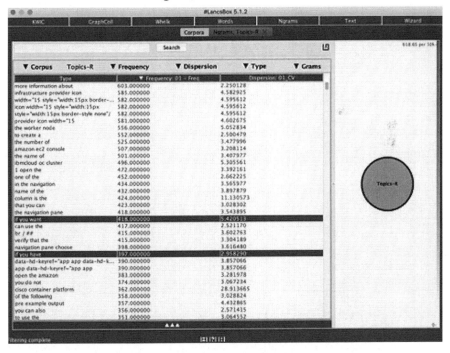

*Figure 5.4. 3-gram analysis of a product documentation
corpus showing frequent use of "if you" phrases.*

The 3–gram analysis may be enough to either confirm a theoretical understanding or provide grounds for developing a theory, perhaps about how contingent or hypothetical contexts are used for addressing users of documentation.

Findings from a word or keyword analysis may also be used in conjunction with N-gram analysis. While Lancsbox and other tools allow searching for keywords in an N-gram analysis, AntConc allows such searching using the Cluster analysis. Either way, such functions will help build a better sense of what is happening around those keywords.

Unlike the keyword in context (KWIC) analysis, the N-gram analysis shows not just the variety of contexts across which the keyword appears but also the larger units of discourse to which that keyword is attached. For example, in a study of product documentation, a word-level analysis might show the prevalence of terms indicating hypothetical circumstances (e.g., if, unless, should, etc.). A KWIC analysis could then show the variety of places where these terms are used (see Figure 5.5.). For example, an N-gram analysis might show that there are some phrases that are more common (e.g., "if you want to" or "unless you have") which then provide more insight about what the participants are writing and talking about. Through the N-gram search depicted in Figure 5.5, we can discover other forms of hypothetical constructions around the pronoun "you," including "if you" and "you can."

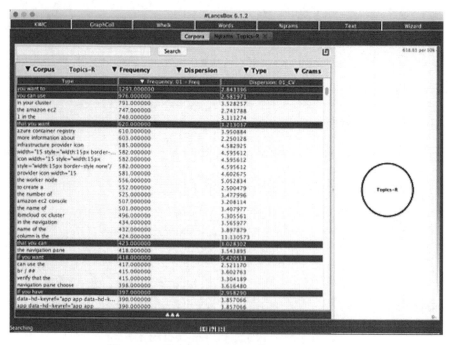

Figure 5.5. N-gram search on "you" in a product documentation corpus to find hypothetical phrases.

Visual Collocation Analysis

Some corpus analysis tools support visualizations showing patterns of word use that can be helpful for confirming a theory or developing a new one. In AntConc, the visualization is called a concordance plot, and it shows dispersion of a key term throughout a corpus. Lancsbox offers a visualization tool called graph collocation that allows a search of words to show a network of connections that the word has to others in the corpus. The visualization that it produces (Figure 5.6) is a network of relationships showing:

- **Strength**: how often the words are connected
- **Distance**: how many words intervene between the graphed terms
- **Location**: where the words are connected (i.e., to left or right of a search term)

The result is a visualization of words that flow into each other and (perhaps commonly) appear together. From a network perspective, those clustered words might appear to circulate around a common concept.

In Figure 5.6, the visualization shows words associated with the mention of "you" in apology letters and how those words link (e.g., via "to, with, for, the, this, that") to words associated with "our" in those letters. The collocation may give us a picture of actions associated with the letter recipients versus those associated with the letter writers.

From the standpoint of convention analysis, a graphic visualization of collocations can show us conventional ways that letter recipients are addressed in apology letters. If the corpora we have includes sample letters from business communication textbooks and apology letters in the wild, we may gauge how closely CEOs are following conventions expressed in textbooks. If there is divergence between word use in the two corpora, it may be worth exploring.

Depending on the size of the corpus, a graphic visualization of word associations might be too jumbled to be much good for analysis. To mitigate this problem, make adjustments to the thresholds for strength of associations and frequency of associations to show only strong connections.

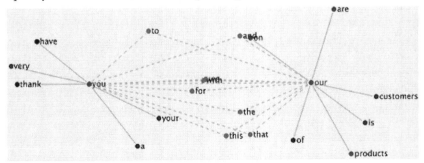

Figure 5.6. Output from Graph Collocation in Lancsbox.

▉ Dispersion Analysis

All of the functions described above are useful at either finding evidence to support or refine a deductive analysis of your data. They are also good at exploring the data, as might be done in an approach leading up to the creation of theory or practical applications. If all things come together and the data align, you will soon arrive at ideas or conclusions that appear to be supported by the data. Before you jump from that data to a close reading, however, there is one additional analysis that may be warranted: dispersion analysis.

Dispersion analysis can help assure that what is revealed in the quantitative analysis is characteristic of the data and not a rare language phenomenon. In different tools, dispersion analysis may be called distribution, range, or other something else. As we discussed in the above section on word and keyword analysis, it may even be possible to find information on dispersion with those functions. Either way, the point is to use a dispersion function to check that a phenomenon is relatively widespread in the data set.

In Lancsbox, the tool for supporting dispersion analysis is the Whelk tool. This tool allows you to search a word (or a word plus its part of speech) to determine how frequently it appears and across how many texts in the corpus. As with the word/keyword analysis, the results are a figure ranging from zero (even dispersion) to larger numbers reflecting increasingly uneven dispersion. The function will also produce box plots showing where a term appears more prominently in the corpus. Focusing on words with even dispersion is good for understanding a corpus' potentially distinctive and patterned use of words. Investigating unevenly distributed words may allow you to identify meaningfully unique texts or determine that some texts are outliers skewing the representativeness, balance, or diversity of your corpus.

Returning to the example corpus of group collaboration, we might use a dispersion analysis to test emerging interpretations of the data. If we found that a sub-corpus of groups following one kind of collaboration methodology used more question words (e.g., what, which, when, etc.) we might interpret the finding to mean that those group members are doing more to create a shared sense of purpose and aims. However, if a dispersion analysis showed us that most of the question words were used by only a subset of groups within the corpus, the data point would be less convincing. In that case, the use of questions words might say something more about the groups who use it rather than the collaboration methodology used by all groups in the sub-corpus.

Even with an overview of the analytic options in tools like AntConc and Lancsbox, it can be challenging to link questions (Chapter 3) to the tools that assist in answering them. Choosing an appropriate tool starts with understanding your analytic approach. You need to decide whether to build up to a theory through cumulative analysis of samples (induction) or to use theory to predict patterns of language use (deduction). Each approach points to different tools.

Assisted Inductive Approaches

There will be times in your investigation of corpora when the purpose of your research is to determine whether two corpora are similar or different. Going back to our hypothetical corpus of collaborative meetings, we might suppose that our groups differ on how they collaborate and that the format of their meetings (i.e., in person, online, hybrid) is associated with changes in those collaboration activities. If we were to interpret collaboration through a theoretical framework, like "communities of practice" (Wenger, 1998), the theory could provide clues about what activities to look for in the discourse. This kind of starting point is ideal for inductive approaches to data analysis. It is not our purpose in this chapter to walk through the process of inductive analysis, however. There are plenty of other resources that take such an explanation as their express purpose (e.g., Charmaz, 2014; Glaser, 1965; Krippendorff, 2018). Instead, our purpose is to show how you might use concepts and techniques of corpus analysis (Chapter 2) to engage with the inductive questions.

Questions like those of kind, dispersion, association, time, and meaning (Chapter 3) share a similar quality in that they support exploratory research. Questions of kind ask what something is. Questions of dispersion ask where lexical and grammatical features are spread out in a corpus. Questions of association and time ask how those lexical and grammatical features are associated with one another and arranged in time. Questions of meaning ask about the characteristics that make one corpus different from another.

Intuition, experience, and hunches might give you some starting points for analyzing these questions. For this reason, you may want to jump into the data, assess what is there, and take notes as you go. The result of this exploration may be that you develop a theory that can be confirmed through more focused investigation of the data. Any subsequent understanding of the discourse can then be developed by doing a systematic analysis, word by word and phrase by phrase, to build up a set of possibilities for describing the phenomenon under investigation. For example, a notion that a phenomenon of interest in the corpus is related to cohesion in regulatory writing might lead us to look at cohesion-building words, search for conjunctions as a part of speech, seek indexing words that are typically inserted by writers to give guidance to readers, or identify patterns of metadiscourse. The published literature in language analysis, linguistics, and English for specialized purposes often yields helpful, close analyses of word type and word structures. These can help guide analysis. Simple descriptive analyses such as those supported by frequency counts, proportional ranges, and dispersion ratings (Chapter 2) can indicate whether those aspects might distinguish corpora. Of course, some search results will lead to dead ends, but some will likely point to meaningful places to explore further.

This initial exploration phase can help you zoom in on the qualities that might be pivotal in describing the corpus and may help you find language features that become distinctive in their association with other variables. For example, finding that a corpus of official press releases from a city has a high proportion of "to be" verbs might indicate passive voice. If those passive voice indicators are associated with fewer than expected personal pronouns, you might be onto clues about how writers are developing different stances toward the claims the city's representatives are making.

At this point in your analysis, you may start using terms like "high" and "low" and "expected" versus "unexpected" to describe the frequencies of words and phrases in your corpus. Although these might seem like subjective terms, they can be built on mathematical predictions about how language content is expected to be distributed in a corpus of a given size. Most unaided researchers will not be able to do much more than intuit a sense of what constitutes "high/low" or "expected/unexpected." Corpus analysis tools, however, can compare corpora head-to-head and determine the expected dispersion of language content. You can then compare those expectations to actual computations on the corpus or corpora you are using. The result will be an indication of "high/low" or "expected/ unexpected" frequency of words. After you determine whether these assessments are accurate or based on tabulation errors (e.g., double counting homophones, not counting contractions) they can give you a sense of what findings might be worth pursuing.

Furthering the work of inductive exploration, you could use features of analytic techniques that examine language diversity. Your corpora may be tallied in terms of tokens (discrete appearances of a single word), but you may also investigate different lemmatizations of the words that appear to be interesting. For example, in a corpus of white papers from a tech organization, we might want to look at verbs used to make claims. We could do a frequency analysis of verbs to determine whether verbs like "argue," "claim," "assert," "believe" are more or less prevalent in different corpora. A proportion analysis could tell us what proportion of the verb set is accounted for with each verb under investigation. Furthermore, a collocation analysis could lead us to investigate the nouns that follow those verbs. Is this company making explicit arguments in their white papers? If so, what is the company arguing about? Is there a relationship between the kinds of things that the company makes firmer arguments about (e.g., as indicated in words like "assert" or modals of certainty like "will") versus those that they make hedged arguments about (e.g., as indicated by words like "claim" or modals of uncertainty like "could")? These kinds of inquiries tell us something about the argumentative actions taken and about the diversity of the argumentative actions expressed. By tracking lemmatized forms of different verbs (e.g., argue, argued, argues, arguing, argumentation, argument), we can see the diversity of ways that a term might be used in the corpus and how the company may be making (or avoiding making) direct arguments about the topics of the white papers.

Questions of meaning can be answered in similar ways to those we have been discussing. Frequencies, proportions, dispersion rates, and measures of linguistic diversity will give us some composite picture of a corpus as a whole. However, other functions like keyword analysis and associated keyness measures like log-likelihood and chi square will speak more directly to the different meanings (or aboutness) in the corpora being compared (Chapter 2). Keyness analyses can reveal content-laden words that may be important for driving further inductive analysis of the corpus. For example, a keyness analysis of our fictional corpus of collaborative meetings might reveal that there are differences in the type verbs used and, consequently, in the kinds of collaborative actions members of those groups are undertaking. Such a finding would be a solid piece of evidence in saying how the corpora differ and how collaborations held in person, online, or in a hybrid format differ from each other.

Questions of association and time are those that we can ask in a similar exploratory manner. Once we start to develop awareness of the language in use, we can test assumptions by looking for collocations of terms that we expect to find near each other in the data set. We can also start to look for clusters of words that appear around words of interest. Functions like keyword in context (KWIC), collocation analysis, and graph collocations can allow exploration of gradually larger units of discourse. In the case of our corpus of collaborative meetings, we might use collocation analysis to observe that different verbs are associated with different ends (e.g., build agreement, create a common focus, align goals, etc.). And a dispersion analysis might show us where and how those verbs cluster in a meeting. Do certain kinds of actions (as instantiated in repeated words) tend to occur at the beginning, middle, or end? Before or after other kinds of actions? Further, we can look at clusters of words around those verbs to identify what other verbs are connected to the target verbs or what kinds of conjunctions are used to link arguments together. Gradually, this expanding exploration of a corpus through questions of association will add more information to the theoretical framework and potentially lead to cohesive theories that can drive specific investigation of the data set.

The important point at this stage in the analysis is to keep good notes. Good notes document patterns that you expected and found, patterns that you expected to find but did not, and surprise findings. The surprises might turn out to be meaningful if you can explain or otherwise account for them within the theoretical framework you started from. The initial data may also give reason to revise a theoretical framework to better account for the data being uncovered.

Based on the descriptive work done with inductive approaches to questions of kind, dispersion, meaning, association, and time, you might further develop the theoretical framework so that it becomes possible to advance a theory about what may be going on in a corpus. At that point, you can track how language variables may verify that theory.

Some researchers might simply begin from this point and engage with corpora with theories in mind about what they might see. For these researchers, deductive approaches to the investigation might be more appropriate.

■ Assisted Deductive Approaches

Unlike inductive approaches, deductive approaches will proceed from a theory to apply a framework of analysis to the data in the corpus. Approaching a corpus deductively means that we are approaching it with some kind of analytic structure in mind that gives shape to the data before we encounter it. So, while frequency counts, proportion analysis, dispersions, and collocations are still valuable, the exploratory work that they afford may need to be redirected toward a theory that is being tested.

Questions of meaning, use, identity, and convention (Chapter 3) especially are those that might require a deductive approach to corpus analysis. These questions are more likely to derive from a theory about what is going on in the corpus, but they need not be so driven. These questions build up from simpler base questions—like questions of association and time—but seek to ascribe more specific meaning and significance to the patterns researchers find. Ultimately, questions of meaning, use, identity, and convention are looking for features in the corpora under investigation as well as associations between those features. But researchers will need to ascribe meaning to those features through coding. We talk more about coding below.

When testing a theory, it can be helpful to use annotations (Chapter 4). Structural annotations can be particularly helpful, for example, in dividing a corpus into segments or units of analysis that the literature may suggest are important. Segmenting data is a purposeful way of dividing your data into cohesive units of information that will help isolate a phenomenon of interest (Geisler & Swarts, 2019).

Segmentation can use grammatical, topical, or structural units. By dividing data into these units ahead of time, you can more easily get a count of the linguistic features you are interested in tracking, with proportions scaled to your unit of segmentation. For example, if we had a corpus of technical descriptions, written by experienced and inexperienced writers, such as might be used for developing a training curriculum, we could choose to segment the technical descriptions in the corpus in different ways to generate different kinds of insights. We might segment the papers according to structural properties in accordance with genre-based approaches to studying such descriptions (e.g., Pflugfelder, 2017). By segmenting texts into conventional sections, we might more readily track rhetorical moves. Or we might take theories related to search and information foraging (e.g., Erickson, 2019; Pirolli, 2007) and segment out introductory clauses to study their pragmatic function (i.e., questions of use) for guiding readers to the content they may be seeking.

When comparing frequency lists and collocations of words in a corpus, many corpus analytic tools will support statistical analysis of those features. Measures such as t-tests can tell if the corpora being examined are significantly different from one another. Chi square can provide some insight about how likely it is that some linguistic variables found in a target corpus are going to vary systematically between the target and reference corpora. The data from these analyses can usually be exported to spreadsheets as a list of comma- or tab-separated values that can then be used to support additional statistical analysis. Some tools, like Lancsbox, support statistical analysis directly in the interface. Further discussion of the statistical tests is beyond the scope of this volume, and thus readers are directed to textbooks such as Brezina's *Statistics in Corpus Linguistics: A Practical Guide* (2018). Brezina's volume helpfully covers statistical measures and how to understand their significance. Additional support from traditional statistics textbooks may also be helpful.

With these types of analysis, you may have enough structure to push forward on a theoretical examination of corpora. However, you may also need to dive a little deeper by pulling out samples of the discourse for closer inspection through qualitative means. Distant readings supported through corpus analysis do not obviate the need for close, qualitative readings. Often to get at questions of meaning, use, and convention, we need to understand the nuance of what people are saying or writing. We need to get in and code the data, but in a way that is informed by the patterns of language use that we can identify through corpus analytic means. Through our distant readings, we will develop a sense of what variables are worth viewing closer based on their evenness of dispersion, frequency of appearance, or the statistical likelihood that those variables are pointing to qualities that characterize or differentiate corpora. And this is the object of the final section of this chapter.

▋ Limitations of Distant Reading

It is more difficult to draw large-scale, forward-looking implications from a distant reading study than it is from a close-reading study. It may seem ironic that quantitative, generalizable results often cannot easily be turned into large-scale, forward-looking results, but results of this type run squarely into the is-ought problem. Distant readings can tell the researcher what is in the corpus, but it is not easy to jump from what is to what ought to be done as a result of what is.

Instead, distant readings function best when answering discrete questions. The discrete questions should be written in such a way as to interrogate open questions formed by the literature review. If that is the case, then the literature may help extend the findings from what is to what ought to be. But the findings alone cannot speak to what ought to be, without further analysis, and for that we may need to study samples of the data up close.

▋ Take a Sample

After using these different analyses, you should have a good sense of what you are looking at in your data. The quantitative analysis supported by the tools will give you a feel for what kinds of patterns you have in the data and how common they are. Some studies with research questions that function like hypotheses will be primarily finished at this point. A final step for these studies often includes finding examples that depict the findings of the quantitative analysis.

For those whose research questions are more oriented toward exploratory or open-ended results, the next step is the most critical part of the analysis process. You will have a sense of not only what is in the data but whether what you are finding is "significant" enough (e.g., frequent, prominently located) to support a close reading of examples. Now is when you switch back from the distant reading of the corpus to a close reading of examples from the corpus in a sample (Figure 5.7).

It is important to note here that sampling a population as discussed in Chapter 4 and sampling the corpus as described here are actions that take place in different phases of the research process. While both actions require choosing a smaller set of things from the whole (which is why they both use the verb "sample" in their terminology), sampling a population is part of the corpus building process and sampling examples from the corpus is part of the analysis process.

Most corpus analysis tools will support creating a sample from texts in the corpus and will often allow you to download a sample of data in CSV format. If you know the patterns you are interested in analyzing, you can take a sample of text that adequately represents those patterns. While your qualitative analysis might rely on further coding, the conclusions you draw about an entire corpus from a representative sample are highly likely to be representative of the corpus and internally valid.

Many resources detail aspects of coding, and we refer readers to these (e.g., Saldaña, 2016, which both Stephen and Jason have used). We will conclude by saying that, based on your engagement with your data, you will likely have a sense of what you want to code and what those phenomena look like in the data. You will be able to write a code definition to apply to the ideas and concepts drawn from your corpus analysis techniques in the sample of data. If you chose to use representational annotations while cleaning your data, these representational annotations may help you guide your coding (Chapter 4). If you chose to use inferential annotations, the codes you create now will differ from, but may build on, the inferential annotations.

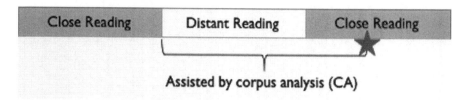

Figure 5.7. The move back to close reading.

The amount of data that you want to pull from your corpus is not fixed, and there is some disagreement about how much to take. We feel that 10 percent of the data that represent the phenomenon you are intending to study is a good place to start. You can pull a random sample from your corpus or use other sampling strategies to identify a portion of data. Once you have sampled your corpus, you can examine and mark up the texts in your sample with your codes. You should then verify that coding with a second coder to ensure the accuracy of your coding and the intuitiveness of your coding scheme.

The result will be data that you can describe both in terms of its lexical/grammatical features and dispersions of coded words throughout the corpus that reflect elements of the discourse in the corpus. Findings derived from these techniques will be nuanced and close to the language, while also informed in broad ways by observations of the language patterns visible from a distance. This is how we analyze text at scale.

Moving between theory informed by close engagement with texts to descriptions of language phenomena that illustrate those theories across a corpus is the process of corpus analysis. These types of analysis can produce results that technical communication needs, especially now that the field has matured and acquired so much academic and industry-specific content. Corpus analysis can help further research in technical communication and create grounds upon which further studies can be developed. Chapter 6 will offer an example study of how those levels of research engagement might work.

6. Writing the Results

The purpose of this chapter is to reflect on the process of conducting and reporting a corpus analysis. We will address a large-scale, exploratory question about technical communication style using techniques of corpus analysis. After introducing the question, we set it into a context that illustrates the value of corpus analysis in addressing the question. Next, we present the results of the corpus analysis and interweave meta-cognitive discussion of the methodological decisions that sit behind those results. The result is a reflective demonstration of a mixed quantitative/qualitative corpus analysis. The chapter is not intended to stand as a typical research report. Instead, it is more transparent about methodological and analytical decisions, as well as dead ends that might otherwise happen off stage in a published account.

The Register of Topic-Based Writing

Biber et al. outline various research objectives that may be suited to corpus analysis. One is register analysis: the study of language that is specific to a situation (2000). A register might belong to a specific social group, and it may be a way of enacting identity, expressing values, or accomplishing something (see Gee, 2005, pp. 11–13).

As an object of study, however, a register is an object with fuzzy borders. Individual uses of language (whether in text or speech) are reflective of the register; however, an analyst might not recognize characteristics of the register without first seeing multiple instances of use. Corpus analysis can provide a good initial picture of the register that can drive closer analysis.

Technical communication has its own questions about register. One set of questions concerns modular or topic-based writing (see Andersen, 2013; Andersen & Batova, 2015b; Baker, 2013; Hackos & IBM, 2006). Topic-based writing is produced in small, conceptually independent pieces that can be combined with other topics and outputted to different formats (e.g., procedures or marketing collateral). Well-written topics have content that is easily repurposed and shared across topics.

We consider topic-based writing to be a socio-technical register created as a result of interacting with structured authoring technologies in organizations that value efficient construction and reuse of content. The question is: what constitutes a topic? And what does the register of topic-based writing look like, in aggregate, as a cohesive set of stylistic practices? As valuable as this question may be, it is difficult to answer without taking a broad look at the various ways that topic-based writing has been implemented and developed as a register. Taking such a broad look at a writing practice entails looking at a large number of texts, more than could be processed manually without overlooking trends or artificially amplifying the features of the few texts that can be inspected manually. For this reason, corpus analysis is a good methodological choice in this case.

Getting started on a corpus analysis, we need to develop awareness of what our language phenomenon looks like. If we consult the published literature on topic-based writing, we find many descriptions of topic-based writing. Among the more common descriptors are notes that topics are:

- "designed to stand on their own with cross-references to other topics" (Rockley, Manning & Cooper, 2009, p. 4);
- "discrete piece[s] of content that [are] about a specific subject, [have] an identifiable purpose, and can stand alone" (p. 24);
- written to "answer a single question" (p. 46); or
- are self-contained and contain no necessary links to other content (Bellamy, Carey & Schlotfeldt, 2012, p.18)

Although descriptive, these definitions do not provide much insight about the uses of topics or how topics should be crafted to best suit those purposes. Topics will vary in size and granularity, depending on the contexts in which they are used. But writing them well always depends on understanding how they are to be used. For example, how do writers rely on topics to build relationships with readers? Answering a large-scale question like this requires what Mueller described as a distant analysis that yields a sketch or an overview of a complex phenomenon (2019).

To get this big picture, we could examine how writers are advised to create topics. To the extent that there are consistencies in what writers are advised to do and consistencies in the way they enact that advice, we may find patterns of language use across examples that sketch a picture of that topic-based register. Concretely, writers are advised to avoid including:

- metadiscourse;
- pointing, sequential language; and
- product-specific information (Bellamy et al., 2012)

Notice that the focus is on what topics lack, which does not leave readers with a clear sense of what this register is or does. However, we can design a corpus analytic approach that will provide us with the overview of what a topic-focused register does. We can interpret that description in light of what we know writers are attempting to do with their topics: for example, create an informative user experience for readers. Addressing this exploratory question requires us to review more of what we know about topics, and develop inquiries that derive from understanding the challenges addressed by topic-based writing and the problems with user experience created as a result.

◼ Literature Review: What We Know about Topics

To understand topic-based writing as a register, we first need context to understand why people write topics. The organizational and professional context of topic-based writing will make clear what topics are intended to do. This knowledge will then help us choose how to apply corpus analytic techniques to describe the register and to identify typified contributions from writers of topics.

Topic-based writing is a form of technical communication that has emerged at the meeting point between concerns over user engagement with technical content, organizational pressure for greater efficiency and effectiveness of documentation practices, and the availability of authoring and archiving technologies that enable the storage and concatenation of raw content. These circumstances create the conditions for a register of technical discourse to arise, but it comes with user experience issues (e.g., orientation and navigation). The resulting topic-based registers that writers have developed over time can show us ways of addressing these user experience issues that can be taught to other writers.

One thread of this discussion on topic-based writing can be traced to concerns about user engagement with documentation and the challenges of converting documentation into action (e.g., Paradis, 1991). A significant part of the underlying problem of converting documentation to action is that readers do not always engage with the documentation; they read just enough to get by (Redish, 1989) or read just enough to think that they can get by.

John Carroll homed in on problems like these and found, at heart, a "paradox of sense-making," which states that

the problem is not that people cannot follow simple steps; it is that they do not . . . People are always already trying things out, thinking things through, trying to relate what they already know to what is going on, recovering from error. In a word, *they are too busy learning to make much use of the instruction.* (1990, p. 74)

Instruction that is too rigid gets in the way because it asserts too much control or makes too many presumptions about the reader's circumstances for learning, such that the instruction cannot be readily adapted (see Swarts, 2018). As theorized, topics are potentially free(er) of constraining context and presumptions about the circumstances in which they are read.

The connection between the paradox of sense-making and more modern practices of topic-based writing is clear to someone like Carlos Evia, who identifies the development and popularization of minimalist approaches to documentation as a driver of topic-based authoring strategies, content management systems, and the development of information models like the Darwin Information Typing Architecture, or DITA (2018). As a register, topic-based writing addresses user engagement by limiting content to "reduce the interference in a user understanding content" (Gillespie, 2017, p. 2).

The core problem that Carroll recognized in documentation was that it was too specific and too controlling of a reader's experience. It was not flexible enough to allow adaptation of the content to the users' circumstances of use, which is what readers want to do with that information (Redish, 1993). Documentation cannot get by with providing readers precise plans or a set of presumptive circumstances under which to interpret and use that content because plans have to give way to situated actions when readers attempt to apply lessons from documentation within their use situations (see Suchman, 2007).

The solution to the paradox of sense-making is loosely structured documentation with more gaps between topics and less control language that links topics together in specific and necessary ways. The change to "minimalism" results in topics with less restrictive meanings and a greater number of potential meanings, making the content adaptable to different contexts. Adaptability to context continues to be one of the aspirational goals of well-developed topics (see Eble, 2003; Flanagan, 2015).

Nudging topic-based writing in the same direction are organizational forces that are interested in making documentation more efficient and effective. Moves toward standardization of content that gave rise to modern organizations (e.g., Rude, 1995; Yates, 1993) favored writing that was standardized and predictable. Writing that has less control language and fewer words that assume or shape a reader's experience is also easier to reuse across different organizational contexts (see Hackos & IBM, 2006; O'Neil, 2015).

The picture of topic-based writing so far shows attempts to engage readers by assuming less about their circumstances and motivation for reading. Topics are the granular pieces of content that support readers by allowing them to follow documentation in any given direction from any starting point. Topics neither assume a reader has read anything before that point nor assume that a reader will read any particular thing afterward. As Mark Baker describes it, every page is (or should be) page one (Baker, 2013).

Practitioners of topic-based writing have developed standards for addressing the problems of communicating linearly-structured text in non-linear ways. These attempts are particularly important given the widespread adoption of the DITA information model and the subsequent development of the model into lightweight, more easily learned versions of the standard (Evia, 2018). Authors of topic-based writing would, in some way, attempt to help readers understand the content without needing the surrounding context.

Readers who can use these cues to understand topic-based writing are "qualified" readers, ones "who [know] everything needed to perform the specific and limited purpose of the topic except the specifics of the case that the topic covers" (Baker, 2013, p. 127). The qualified reader is knowledgeable and has background information necessary to understand the topic or to take steps to make themselves qualified by acquiring the knowledge necessary to process information supplied in a topic (p. 156). Skilled practitioners of a topic-based writing register would, we might intuit, attempt to help readers become qualified. They might help readers build coherent connections between topics without creating obligatory coherent connections between topics using control language. And this intuition, derived from the literature, helps us decide on language features worth tracking across examples of the discourse.

Topic-based writing has been around as a concept at least since Robert Horn and colleagues theorized and experimented with writing that utilized repeated block structures dynamically linked though information maps (Horn et al., 1969). One of the most influential drivers of contemporary topic-based writing as an industry standard was the development of DITA by IBM between the late 1990s and early 2000s. Using the DITA information model directly leads to the articulation of a topic as a kind of standalone content, the structure of which is defined by the DITA information model (Evia, 2018, p. 9). The topic and attendant writing styles attempt to solve the problem of writing content that was intended for linear delivery (e.g., as a chapter):

Information written for a linear structure tends to explicitly receive the strand of meaning from the preceding subject and pass the strand to the next one. This type of information also often refers to more distant subjects within the same linear structure (Priestley et al., 2001, p. 353)

Priestley et al. point toward the concept of coherence with this statement, suggesting that text builds focus as it flows from one point to the next. But in the context of topic-based writing, which is not written in one-to-the-next style, what does coherence look like? What aspects of topic-based writing assist with coherence for the reader? We can assume that as writers have figured out how to assist readers at finding coherence between topics when working with DITA and other information models for topic-based authoring. It is also a reasonable assumption that the techniques that writers use in topic-based writing differ from those used in documentation written prior to the adoption of information models like DITA.

As used in this analysis, coherence should be understood as a way of building focus and conceptual linkages between topics or as the ability to link ideas together in the way presumed of qualified readers. As topics have become more standalone and disconnected from obligatory connections to other topics that complete a broader context concerning a subject, writers still need to accommodate the readers who must recover some of this broader context. If topic-based writing styles have developed to accommodate these kinds of readers, we might expect to find some cues in the writing that assist with coherence/context building without over-specifying the links and grounding the topics into a necessary, linear relationship.

Research on coherence points to the words we use to signal relationships between ideas. These strategies could be as simple as sequencing language and other forms of metadiscourse that indicate relationship structures like "first, second, third" that signal sequence. Phrases like "as mentioned previously" indicate sequence and a relationship between topics. More subtle language cues like pronoun use and the use of determiners like "this" and "that" indicate context by pointing readers back into a text or forward into a text toward the concept to which the pronoun or determiner points (Halliday, 2004). Still more subtle ways of signaling coherence come through sentence structures and sentence rhythms, like using "given to new" structures to show a relationship between ideas (Halliday, 2004; Williams, 1997). We can also signal coherence structurally. Jan Spyridakis studied structural elements in writing and found that elements like headings, previews, and logical connector language helps readers with inference and recall tasks (1989). The lesson is that literature on linguistics and language use will provide evidence of linguistic structures that are associated with the rhetorical effect we want to track in our corpus. Such research will allow us to formulate testable research questions.

Given the spare nature of topic-based writing, it is likely that not many explicit coherence markers are going to be present to link between topics. The structures might very well be more subtle and rely on subtle differences in function language: "words, including pronouns, prepositions, articles, and a small number of similar short but common words" that link together ideas but generally pass below readers' direct level of awareness (Pennebaker, 2011, p. 22). These subtle language choices may have big cumulative effects that contribute to readers' awareness of linkages or other cognitive structures that imply relationships between topics.

Ted J. Sanders et al. (1992) demonstrate that coherence can be built up by tapping into readers' understanding of cognitive primitives that allow them to intuit associations between ideas and topics (p. 6). For example, writers can use words like "if" and "then" to signal a causal relationship. Other language in the same topic might indicate where cause or effect is located (back in the text or forward in the text) (Sanders et al., 1992). The language could also signal polarity (i.e., positive or negative) (Sanders et al., 1992). The subtlety of these language choices already suggests that seeing patterns will be difficult. Some computer-assistance could be helpful at identifying how topics differ or match each other based on a language use pattern that might escape casual and small-scale analysis of a handful of topics. Corpus analysis can help reveal patterns and assist us in finding examples of the broader register to study in closer detail.

To illustrate, we will use corpus analysis to do two things. First, we will use it to test an intuition about topic-based writing, which is that it does not include (or has less) control language that creates obligatory connections between topics. Thus, the first question:

- Do corpora of topic-based writing and traditional (book-based) writing differ in the amount of control language used?

The second question gets at the second intuition: writers of topic-based documentation will attempt to help readers find information to help them become the qualified readers that topics assume them to be.

- How do corpora of topic-based writing and book-based writing differ in their use of language that could be attributed to building a sense of coherence?

■ Methods

The literature provided us with ideas for how to create our study, contrast corpora, and query the corpora to find answers to our two research questions about register. We can now take the next methodological steps. In the sections that follow, we discuss building corpora to highlight the register we want to study and we discuss how to choose an analytic approach based on the literature review.

▌ Data Collection and Corpus Creation

In the case of topic-based versus book-based writing, our contrast is built into the inquiry. One corpus will be a collection of documents written by people who follow a topic-based writing approach and the other corpus will be a collection of documents written by people who follow more of a book-based approach. To find samples of these kinds of discourse, we queried populations of practicing technical communicators.

Jason sent a survey to local chapters of the Society for Technical Communication (STC) and to alumni of technical communication programs[5] asking participants to identify with either of these two descriptions:

- "I produce 'topic-based writing' which consists of standalone topics (i.e., content chunks) that can be reused in different contexts."
- "I produce 'book-oriented writing' (or document-oriented writing) which consists of content designed for a singular use and context of delivery (e.g., a user manual)."

Thirty-five writers responded to the survey. Forty-nine percent (17) produced "topic-based writing" (TW), 34 percent (12) produced "book-based writing" (BW), and 17percent (6) produced both. Writers of both topic-based and book-based writing directed Jason to examples of documentation. These initial sets of documentation formed the seeds for the two corpora: topic-based and book-based.

Jason downloaded samples of the files and stored them in a format readable by corpus analysis software (Lancsbox). He then spot-checked the samples within each corpus to determine that they had the surface appearance of being topic-based, according to guidelines outlined in the literature reviewed in the previous section. The size of these corpora was sufficiently large that only spot-checking the files was feasible, but all of those author-supplied pieces appeared to be correctly identified. Similarly, the book-based writing also appeared consistent as a corpus.

Another issue in corpus creation is balance. Where one samples from within a given set of discourse can influence the analysis. If the selection criteria

---

5. IRB exempt.

overemphasize a particular kind of text or text feature, then that corpus might not adequately represent the expected range of discourse. To address balance in both the topic-based and book-based writing corpora, we included whole documentation sets, including appendices. For topic-based writing, doing so entailed either obtaining PDFs of the whole documentation set or saving each topic from the documentation set accessed online. With full documentation sets, we could be sure to have all kinds of documentation topics represented proportionally. No particular feature or section (beginning, middle, or end) would be emphasized more than another.

An early problem with sample collection for the two corpora was the limited availability of book-based samples. Jason found additional samples of book-based writing by searching for documentation sets circulated as PDF prior to widespread adoption of information modeling standards used in modern topic-based writing. This consisted of documentation published before 1995, spot checked for consistency with other book-based documentation sets. The search was limited to PDF versions of software and hardware documentation that could be obtained through a time-constrained internet search (i.e., return all values before 1995). In the end, the result was two corpora:

- Topic-based Writing: 1,344 files (i.e., topics) representing 6,519,854 tokens
- Book-based Writing: 124 files (i.e., complete documentation sets) representing 3,546,590 tokens

Tokens are strings of letters separated from each other by white space, and in most cases, tokens are equivalent to words. As is clear, the topic-based writing corpus had more of them. The result of this imbalance in token size means that analyses cannot be based solely on word frequencies. Instead, it is better to focus on relative frequencies and better still on measures that account for the disproportionate sizes of the corpora. Lancsbox provides features for doing both.

▮ Analytic Focus

Although the literature on topic-based writing makes it clear that one of the expected differences (compared to book-based writing) would be the lack of control language and the lack of metadiscourse, it was unclear where to start because of the amount of data. Fortunately, corpus analysis software can be quite helpful at exploring a data set. One basic function of corpus analysis software is to determine what words characterize a discourse to get a sense of what could be likely candidates for analysis. Following Scott's (1997) suggestion to get a sense of corpus' "aboutness," an initial approach involves a keyword analysis. During keyword analysis, one compares corpora to determine which words appear with "unusual frequency" (p. 236).

In many cases, someone doing keyword analysis would use a stop list to filter out common words like determiners, prepositions, and conjunctions. In this case, we opted not to filter those terms because this kind of functional language can reveal quite a lot about what language does, in addition to what language says. Our review of linguistic features also suggested that function words like determiners and conjunctions may help build coherence.

A keyword analysis of the topic-based writing corpus yielded mixed results. Words like "api," "platform," "share," "desktop," "server," and "cloud" emerged as highly relevant. However, these mostly content-based words reflected the changing topics of software and hardware documentation over the past 30 years, rather than revealing a change in the register of topic-based writing.

A slightly different way of looking at important words within the corpora is to get a measure of their relative likelihood of occurrence. Log-likelihood gives us a look based on observed frequencies. LogRatio, on the other hand, compares relative frequencies. While it might A slightly different way of looking at important words within the corpora is to get a measure of their relative likelihood of occurrence. Log-likelihood gives us a look based on observed frequencies and their fit with a mathematically derived model of the expected rate of not be a measure of significance, it does say how many times more (or less) likely a term is to appear throughout two different corpora (Hardie, 2014).

LogRatio analysis turns up a more interesting set of function words that started to set topic-based writing apart from book-based writing. Contractions like "what's" and "there's" turn out to be five to six times more likely to appear in topics than in chapters. Words like "there's," "might," "who," and "aren't" are three to four times more likely in topics. Although LogRatio was sensitive to relative frequencies, it is still based on a count of the overall words in the corpus. This function can skew the relative frequency if there is a topic or a handful of topics that account for much of the word usage.

Taking into account dispersion, or the degree to which a word or set of words is used throughout the corpus, we can get a clearer picture of register differences. If one assumes that a discourse feature is characteristic of a register, then it should be somewhat evenly distributed throughout all samples in the corpus.

Using the literature on topic-based writing techniques and the literature on coherence building strategies, we were able to focus on likely linguistic features that distinguish those techniques. The features chosen for analysis were driven by our intuitions about how writers would respond to the demands of addressing "qualified readers" who are presumed to understand enough about a topic's context to understand what they should know in order to use any given topic. Thus, analysis focused on:

- Cohesion relations: words indicating a relationship between ideas (conjunctions, prepositions showing position, prepositions showing composition), and
- Coherence relations: language that disambiguates and creates focus (pronouns, comparative words, determiners, indexicals).

We then prepared strings of words to use as search filters, including those associated with qualities of cohesion and coherence. Using sequences of words culled from grammar books and from discourse analysis resources (e.g., Brown & Yule, 1983), we were able to use the Whelk tool in Lancsbox to determine both the relative frequency of a term and the evenness of its dispersion through the corpus. Words that are relevant to the question (based on the literature), frequently used, evenly distributed, and characteristic of differences between the topic-based and book-based corpora become candidates for analysis.

A similar analysis of control language reveals another set of likely candidates that distinguish book-based from topic-based writing. The literature suggests that positional language —such as "above," "below," "previously," and "ahead"—is one type of control language that guides a reader's experience or assumes a readerly experience that might not be true for someone reading topics out of sequence. In some interpretations of topic-based writing strategies, such words are removed, or their use is curtailed (e.g., Bellamy et al., 2012). Similarly, words like "first," "second," and "lastly" control a reader's experience within a topic. Words like "see" may control experience across topics. The literature on topic-based writing suggests that book-based writing might also have a higher number of pronouns, especially "this," "that," and "it." These pronouns indicate that readers are expected to have encountered the antecedent through the course of linear reading.

Upon finding words that distinguish the corpora, the next step is to draw a better understanding of those function words by examining them in context. The words in isolation may not tell us much about the function they serve. Looking at the keywords in context (KWIC) can show what additional words may be adjacent to the function words and could further elaborate their use in the discourse. A random sample of texts exhibiting the linguistic characteristics identified through analytic filtering of the corpus can then support close qualitative analysis. The results of just such an analysis are presented in the next section.

■ Results

The intent of this analysis is to determine how book-based and topic-based writing differ as registers and to examine how characteristics of topic-based writing might reach out to the "qualified readers" who encounter that documentation. Taking up the first part of this comparison, we focus on how the literature regarding topic-based writing anticipates that it will differ from book-based writing.

If topic-based writing is built from standalone pieces of content that do not make any assumptions about what readers have seen before or after any given topic, then there should be less control language that directs readers to process information in a particular sequence. There may also be less language pointing forward or backward to information that is important to the present discussion but not present in the topic. This is the focus of our first research question: Do corpora of topic-based writing and book-based writing differ in the amount of control language used?

One noticeable way that book-based writing differs from topic-based is in the use of "above" and "below," which are indicative of an assumed reader experience. These prepositions are used frequently in written texts. For example, "see the description of ABC above" or "as seen below, the XYZ."

A KWIC examination of the words "above" and "below" indicates that the two terms are used more often in book-based writing than in topic-based writing. A Welch two-sample t-test of "above" shows a significant difference (t [189.9] = 3.94; p<0.001)[6] with the term appearing more often in book-based writing than in topic-based writing. Likewise, a Welch two-sample t-test of "below" shows a similarly significant difference (t [263.14] = -3.73; p<0.001) with "below" appearing more frequently in book-based writing. Consider Table 6.1.

Table 6.1. Frequencies for "Above" and "Below" in Topic-based (TW) and Book-based (BW) Writing

ID	"Below"	"Above"
BW	1783 (0.001% of the tokens)	1203 (0.0003%)
TW	1698 (0.0002%)	1121 (0.0001%)

Although the raw frequencies look comparable, the mean values are significantly different. That is, because of the difference in size between the corpora, topic-based writing will have more of this kind of control language overall. But if we look at the average rate at which the control language appears in the corpora (in parentheses of the table above), we find that it is used less frequently in topics. Furthermore, we can assess that this language is more evenly distributed in book-based writing:

---

6.   A t-test compares two groups (in this case, of words) by looking at the mean value of the variable we are interested in studying. The "t" value (3.94) represents a ratio of variation between the means of the two groups. In this case, the mean of the group is the average number of times the tested word appears in each of the documents of the group. The t of 3.94 is a high ratio of variation, suggesting that for the two compared groups, the word "above" is statistically far more frequent in one group than the other. (The Welch's version of the t-test is a test that assumes normal distribution of both the compared data sets but allows for the data sets to be different sizes.) The number 189.9 is the degrees of freedom, which is a necessary component with the t value for calculating the p value. The "p" value expresses the likelihood that any variance between the means is statistically significant; the lower the number, the more significant. P values become decreasingly meaningful in the presence of ever-larger amounts of data (Lin et al., 2013), but in some conditions they are still meaningful and/or called for due to concerns about validity of the measures.

- Below: 86 percent dispersion in BW corpus; 21 percent dispersion in TW
- Above: 80 percent dispersion in BW corpus; 18 percent dispersion in TW

This means that 86 percent of the files in the BW corpus include "below" and 80 percent include "above," which strongly suggests that these words are characteristic of BW. Conversely, low levels of dispersion of the terms in TW suggests that these words are not characteristic of TW.

We can also check different measures of dispersion like the coefficient of variance (CV), which measures variation relative to the mean frequency of the word in a corpus. As the number moves closer to zero, the dispersion is more even (Brezina, 2018). In book-based writing, the coefficient of variance for "above" is 1.12 and "below" is 0.88, indicating that neither is completely even in dispersion. However, the range percent (calculated early) shows that they are appearing throughout a majority of files in the corpus. These two analyses together are enough to conclude that the term probably does hint at a register feature. Compare these numbers to the same CV figure in topic-based writing, where "above" only has a CV rating of 3.93 and "below" has a CV of 3.61. Those figures, combined with the low range percent from the previous analysis, supports the expectation that there would be less of this kind of control that presumes a particular kind of reader experience in TW.

Pointing "above" and "below" in a topic makes less intuitive sense to someone accessing topic content non-linearly. The reading experience presumed in words like "above" and "below" is more likely for readers accessing ideas linearly in chapters. Within the context of a single topic, control terms may still be sensible, but the range of possible uses is more constrained. Some examples will illustrate:

- BW #1: "The Filter cell reads the input value, adjusts the output value as described above, and waits an amount of time equal to the Filter Time Period before repeating the process" (Ultrasite)
- BW #2: "For a continuation run, this is done by RESTRT, both for continuing an existing history tape, as described above, and for starting a new tape, as in the branch run" (CCM2 User Guide)[7]

---

7.   In this chapter, many parenthetical citations are references to pieces of data from within the corpus. We are including these references for the purposes of validity and repeatability, not for third-party referencing. If someone sought out our same corpus and ran our study again, the researcher would ideally be able to find that replication of our methods would return the same pieces of data from the corpus that we are reporting here. Given that goal, these citations do not appear in our references section. Generally, this type of corpus content would not be cited in the references section, as corpus data is often complicated to cite or not citable: the documents are often internal, partial, or unpublished data. While the public technical documentation pieces in this analysis are citable, we retain the practice of citing from the corpus for validity's sake and not for referencing's sake.

Both examples show the use of "above" to direct readers to content that they will likely have encountered by the time they read the sections quoted. As such, readers will have the context needed to be qualified readers who understand the reference to that prior knowledge.

Likewise, uses of "below" also indicate that qualified readers are expected to follow up on directives or suspend their questions until reaching the content that completes a point:

- BW #3: "The display modes are described below" (Chem3d)
- BW #4: "see Using an Array Index below" (e-Prime)

Often uses of "below" reference content that immediately follows, but not always. As in these cases, the content readers might need is elsewhere in the documentation, which would cross the dividing line for topics in topic-based writing.

The use of "above" and "below" is less frequent in topic-based writing, and when the words are used, the information referenced as being "above" or "below" is *immediately* above or below and would be contained within the same topic (as opposed to a different section or in an appendix). Redirections to content elsewhere in the documentation is offloaded to the structural and navigational features of the documentation, whether by implicit reference to a specific part of the rhetorical context (e.g., consider the next section) or by explicit use of a redirection link (e.g., a "see also" link).

Our second question asks what topic-based writing does to help readers create coherence (focus) and/or cohesion (flow): How do corpora of topic-based writing and book-based writing differ in their use of language that could be attributed to coherence building? There are likely many ways that topic-based writing is doing both; however, exploration of the data produced a number of dead ends:

- no significant difference in uses of conjunctions across corpora,
- no significant difference in uses of prepositions indicating sequence (first, second, last), and
- no significant difference in uses of phrases indicating cognitive primitive cohesion structures (e.g., if . . . then or because . . . then).

Although one might not normally report exploratory dead-ends in the research process, we include the information to show how corpus analysis does result in some thwarted attempts to find a good language feature for advancing the analysis.

There were no significant differences between the corpora on the word lists generated from the literature on coherence and cohesion, but additional analysis showed that the corpora do differ in their uses of some function words. In particular, conjunctive adverbs, prepositions, determiners, and pronouns are all used to different degrees between book-based writing and topic-based writing. There are too many differences to cover in this analysis, and many do not have clear explanations at this point. However, further analysis of patterns of function words that fit our intuitions about how writers speak to and support "qualified readers" is warranted.

Exploration of prepositions leads to the discovery that "to" was used more frequently in topic-based writing than in book-based writing. By looking more closely at examples of "to" and its context of use, we discovered that "to" often introduced an infinitive phrase. Those infinitive phrases often began sentences, as opposed to appearing as embedded clauses.

An infinitive phrase is grammatically versatile in that it can act as a noun, an adjective, or an adverb while also expressing an action. Infinitives are also used for increasing coherence because they have syntactic functions that are helpful for readers sorting through topics non-linearly:

- Communicating purpose or intention (e.g., "to accomplish this, you must ...")
- Communicating use (e.g., "the 9–digit key is to unlock the secure folder")
- Communicating continuous or ongoing action (e.g., "to configure the storage system") (Education First, 2021)

The infinitives have an agenda-setting function in that they announce a focus for the documentation that follows. It might be "to install," "to migrate services," or something else, but the infinitive orients the reader to the context of action that is assumed. As a subtle signal to readers, the infinitive phrase may be a candidate for a technique of documentation that supports "qualified readers." Infinitive phrases appear in both book-based writing and topic-based writing, but they are more prominently found in topic-based writing.

Lancsbox does not have a direct way of finding infinitive verb phrases, but we can approximate a search by filtering examples of "to" that are followed by a verb. Lancsbox adds annotations for part of speech, which facilitates such an analysis. The result shows both more infinitive phrases in topic-based writing and more stacked or multiple instances of infinitive phrases.

The most common uses of infinitive phrases in both BW and TW are to indicate purpose. They may be used as headings or subheadings to introduce sections of a topic or a chapter. For example:

> TW #1: "**To print** a calendar event
>
> Navigate to calendar and select an event.
>
> Tap the Print icon and follow the same instructions as mentioned in the preceding section To print emails." (Citrix, bold added)

Another example:

> TW #2: "Procedure **to grant** seamless access to an administrator."
> (Druva, bold added)

These examples, some among many, are single uses of infinitive phrases that set up reader expectations about the information that follows. There are similar phrases distributed evenly and widely throughout TW, perhaps because the readers need more statements of purpose. Readers may also need points to draw and keep their attention. Given this finding, we can go back to the literature on "infinitive phrases" to test our interpretation of their use. Is there a case to be made about coherence with infinitive phrases?

▋ Chained/Distributive Linked Topics

If we look further at infinitive phrases in topic-based writing, we find that there are more likely to be stacks of infinitive phrases in topic-based writing in addition to more infinitive phrases than book-based writing. When these infinitives stack, they appear to serve two functions. First, they point out the purpose of a passage. Second, they indicate linked purposes, whether distributively (i.e., chained) or integratively (i.e., embedded), to provide readers with additional guidance to deepen their understanding. Observations like these create opportunities for focused qualitative analysis of passages that use such a pattern of infinitive verbs. A random sampling of content provides the examples we need to make sense of the broader pattern.

The examples of chained topics below show a relationship between linked topics that may spill over the boundaries of a topic:

> TW #3: "If you want **to change** the enforcement setting in specific clients instead of all clients, add or edit the EnableSensorQuarantine setting in the local configuration of those clients (see Tanium Client settings on page 122)" (Tanium).

The subtle function of the infinitive phrase in this passage is that it clarifies the presumed reader motivation ("change").[8] Whether that motivation is preceded by a modal word that indicates conditionality or it is just plainly stated, the infinitive signals that what follows the statement is shaped by, conditioned by, or otherwise mediated by that motivation.

We also find stacked infinitive phrases used to introduce entire instruction sets:

> TW #4: "When an encryption license is used, whether **to encrypt the local data** (user LUs) and the data **to be stored** in the HCP system" (HDI).

---

8. Topics are not always consistent in their avoidance of control language, as evidenced by the notice "(see Tanium Client settings on page 122)." Findings regarding control language in topic-based writing are true as a pattern (even a statistically significant pattern), but not in an absolute sense.

This content appears in a table directing readers to consider different conditions under which they would use the data ingestor (DI). The infinitives are directly used to introduce a conditional set of motivating circumstances: when it is the case that an encryption license is used, a reader should refer to the procedure linked in the column that follows. In this instance, as well as the one before, information clarifies a purpose that is adjacent to the topic but not explicitly addressed. The infinitive completes the thought ("to do X," follow this information), and so it provides information needed by a reader while signaling them to locate this information.

The same kind of chained or distributive use of infinitives appears in situations where the writers signal to readers that there is more than one topic pertaining to the topic being read, and readers are presumed to be familiar with some of those other topics. For example:

> TW #5: "**To address data residency requirements**, it is important **to understand the Hyperledger Fabric architecture** that underlies {{site.data.keyword.blockchainfull_notm}} Platform" (HyperLedger).

The infinitives are used to continue a discussion of remote peers in the discussion of the HyperLedger Platform. The infinitives signal not just a topic that is coming up or a subdivision of the topic at hand, but a concept that is located elsewhere in the documentation. That concept is important enough to be noted in-line.

In the above cases, we find chained uses of infinitives that create connections across conceptually-adjacent topics. Some of these chains link procedures that would be potentially followed in sequence. Others might just link concepts that match procedures to concepts.

These uses of infinitives are not much different in purpose from the use of other contextual markers in texts. The larger presence of infinitive phrasing in TW, however, is unusual in that it results in more language being used to communicate motive. If the user's motives are the same as those anticipated by the topic, the infinitive phrase merely subdivides the content and provides readers with a spot to focus in order to find the information.

Sometimes, topics do not lead off with infinitive phrases or use them as headings to set the purpose of a topic. Instead, the infinitives lay down an information scent that could guide interested users to related information (Pirolli & Card, 1995). For example:

> TW #6: "To design a long running process **to fetch a message and (to) process it,** use Get JMS Queue message activity in a loop instead of Wait For JMS Queue message. In most cases, a JMS starter will be sufficient in this scenario" (TIBCO).

Here the embedded infinitive phrase indicates the relevance of two topics that are elaborated not in the reference topic but elsewhere in the documentation (i.e., Get JMS Queue and Wait for JMS Queue). The chained infinitives have the effect of distributing reader awareness to other topics in the documentation set, even if the readers do not go and find those topics.

Given what we know about the problems associated with navigation and with readers gathering a sense of the rhetorical/functional context of any given topic, it seems like a fair interpretation to consider these uses of infinitives as a corrective to the "lost in the woods" feeling that might inhibit readers from becoming qualified readers.

■ Embedded/Integrative Linked Topics

The integrative use of infinitives also accommodates qualified readers by building a sense of context. However, that context is not of adjacent concepts and processes but of embedded concepts and processes. If chained infinitives expand a sense of context distributively, the integrative uses of infinitives may deepen understanding by embedding motives within actions. Many of these infinitive phrases do not include internal or external links to other topics. Yet they often provide enough information about what qualified readers are expected to know that one could follow up on related topics. For example:

> TW #7: "**To allow Studio to create the database,** click OK. When prompted, click OK, and the database is created automatically. Studio attempts to access the database using the current Studio user's credentials. If that fails, you are prompted for the database user's credentials. Studio then uploads the database schema to the database" (Citrix).

The stacked infinitives at the start of this passage establish a compound motive: to allow Studio to create. This motive leads to the process of carrying the task out. The combined infinitives build an understanding of Studio: it creates the database, but it must be allowed to create the database based on a review of the Studio user's credentials, as we read about in the sentences that follow. Although this passage is somewhat unusual in that it provides an elaboration of the context hinted at in the infinitives, it is an interesting starting point because it shows the depth of the context implied.

Whether Studio creates the database depends on the user's credentials and on the possibility that this Studio user might be different from a database user who has different credentials. The context for this function in Studio relies on an understanding of the organization and the division of labor around the user. We also learn more about Studio in this section. If Studio is allowed access, it will create the database by uploading a database schema. This clarification points to the presence of a database schema, which is part of the topic at hand. None of the implicit references link outward to other sources, but the information pointed to is important for developing an understanding of the process.

In other instances, stacked infinitives play an integrative linking function, and we find references to outside sources and internal sources as well:

> TW #8: "**To instantiate the chaincode,** you need **to send an instantiate proposal**{: external} to the peer, and then send a transaction request{: external} to the ordering service." (v10)

This example is part of a standalone topic on Instantiating a Chaincode. We start with the motive marker "to instantiate the chaincode" and then follow this with another infinitive noting the need "to send an instantiate proposal" and "[to] send a transaction request" ("to" being implied as part of a parallel construction). Instantiating the chaincode is a complicated process that may require users to understand concepts like the "instantiate proposal" and the "transaction request," but the links are not obtrusive and do not insist on readers following them.

Understanding both the "initiate proposal" and the "transaction request" would deepen and improve the reader's understanding of the topic, and both concepts are placed in the context of a broader task. Editing or writing this process would require those people to understand the impacted or related systems. Referencing that context (in this case explicitly) is important for pursuing that deeper understanding.

When stacked infinitive phrases are used in this embedded fashion, it is often to add clarifying context about the process or concept a reader is about to encounter. The infinitives do not always link to or directly point to other topics, but they do give readers a sense of what is expected of them as "qualified readers." For example:

> TW #9: "Add ServiceNow as a destination
>
> **To enable data to be exported to the ServiceNow** CMDB from Asset, enter your ServiceNow Host URL and credentials.
>
> 1. From the Asset menu, click Inventory Management > Destinations.
> 2. Click New Destination > ServiceNow Destination.
> 3. Edit the settings, including the ServiceNow Host URL and credentials, log level, view, and the schedule at which you want the export to occur (Tanium).

The context of this task is to add ServiceNow as a destination. The infinitive phrases clarify what is meant or entailed, which includes enabling data and exporting. These processes do not need additional explanation; they do not link to other related topics on those points. Rather, what the user gets is the understanding that system processing, including enabling and exporting, are related here. The topics to which this passage points are not supplementary to the process, but integral to understanding the process that this procedure is built upon.

■ Conclusion

There are practical implications for this study. Studies like this and others that examine questions of register give practitioners and scholars clues about strategies that we employ for reaching audiences. The findings here confirm that book-based writing does tend to use more control words that make assumptions about what readers have read and can be expected to read. Topic-based writing shows less control language, as expected.

The finding about infinitive phrases does not necessarily mean that writers have consciously adopted a strategy of using them to highlight motives and their related topics. Instead, the finding may indicate that as writers have become accustomed to writing topics, they have developed tacit responses to the challenges their readers face. A close reading of the infinitive phrases used suggests that they certainly do appear capable of helping to establish coherence by building up a sense of context or by laying clues about related topics without requiring the topics.

For practitioners of technical writing, the findings point to the potential impact of choosing function words. If the use of chained and embedded infinitives does serve a navigational and coherence function, it might be worthwhile to deliberately include phrases like this, especially when making implicit references to a broader task context.

Likewise, teachers of technical writing gain the same awareness and sense of importance of infinitives. If there is a use for infinitive phrases, then they might become part of the way that we teach topic-based writing. Infinitives may also become part of the way that we teach how to build navigation, keywords, and other metadata structures to support readers through topic-based documentation. The next step for this investigation may be to test some of these language variables in a usability setting to gauge if there are impacts on navigation.

Questions like those addressed in this study require a scope of analysis that is initially bigger than what one can achieve by looking at examples of texts close up. Without asking broad questions about writing style and looking for language patterns and other syntactic variations across a large body of data, it would be too easy to 1) focus on qualities that appear unusual but might not be representative of the discourse or 2) overlook characteristics of a writing style that only become apparent through computer-assisted ways of looking, ways that do not discount or overlook language that we might find uninteresting or common.

We are scholars of writing. As a result of the many commitments that identity entails, it might seem off-putting to examine discourse only at the computational level. For this reason, it is still vitally important to draw samples from the data to examine more closely, as we do throughout. But instead of examining samples of discourse without a sense of whether those fragments are important, the quantitative analysis shows us the patterns of language use that can guide and contextualize our selection of discourse for analysis.

7. The Future of Corpus Analysis and Technical Communication

We hope that, by this point in the book, the reader considers corpus analysis an achievable and potentially productive method for reflective research in technical communication. The last six chapters have outlined the assumptions, methods, approaches, and limitations of corpus analysis. We believe that scholars and practitioners who understand these concepts will be equipped to produce corpus analysis research that is methodologically sound and makes claims within the bounds of what corpus analysis can effectively support. Furthermore, we hope that the reader will be convinced of the potential that corpus analytic techniques hold not just for furthering the development of technical communication research and practice but for doing so in a way that also looks reflectively at what we have already accomplished and what may have been overlooked. We hope that technical communication scholars and practitioners are ready to add corpus analysis to the list of methodological options for studying and reflecting on the practices of technical communication.

In closing, we turn our attention from the individual corpus analyst to the discipline, because our abilities to advance the goals of technical communication research and practice depend on the disciplinary infrastructures that support them. We call attention to the need for further resources to support corpus analysis in technical communication. Flourishing corpus analysis in the field will require an investment of resources to help ensure that current and future researchers and practitioners can engage in this work. The level of complexity and challenge to attain each of these proposed resources ranges. Some tasks will require a few dedicated individuals to complete, while other initiatives will require contributions from a large number of people across many institutions.

■ Linguistic Knowledge and Resources

A primary need for corpus analysis to flourish in technical communication is linguistic background knowledge, which is needed to engage in corpus analytic work concerning lexical and grammatical features of language. Although linguistic training is not common to technical communication classrooms and trainings, scholars, practitioners, and students of technical communication can acquire an appreciation for the work by examining their own choices. How do we make choices about which words to use, when to modify them, how to indicate stance, and where to signal uncertainty? What do those choices mean about how we build relationships with our readers? What do those word choices say about the training we have received, or about the contexts in which our texts will be used? These kinds of reflective investigations illuminate that lexical and grammatical choices are neither random nor without consequence. And as the studies we have covered in this book show, the lexical choices, grammatical structure, and textual meaning correspond.

Given the presumption that lexical and grammatical choices help signify meaning, interested students and scholars must gain or refresh their knowledge about fundamental lexical and grammatical concepts. These fundamental concepts are necessary to understand the tools of and tutorials about corpus analysis. While we have covered a small number of lexical and grammatical concepts in this book, more work is needed. A short primer on linguistics for technical communication corpus analysis would be a boon to the field in this regard, but books on discourse analysis are very helpful as well (e.g., Gee, 2005; Johnstone, 2017).

Educational Resources: Courses, Workshops, Videos, Textbooks

Corpus analysis is a technology-dependent research approach, and the tools designed to support this research can require a fair amount of technical knowledge. Users of corpus analysis tools, corpus builders, data scrapers, and other adjunct tools can benefit from knowing both how the tool interfaces work but also how the underlying technologies (e.g., optical character scanning, natural language processing, databases, xml coding, regex, etc.) operate. To support this kind of knowledge, the field could use courses and short supplemental instructional content. Such instruction should build awareness of how to use tools with analytic purpose, not simply build tool proficiency.

Time and effort put into corpus analysis education is necessary, and we expect much of it to be done in graduate courses. A 16–week dedicated course on corpus analysis would be a huge benefit to emerging scholars, just as 16–week courses dedicated to ethnography, statistics, or rhetorical analysis are boons to emerging scholars. Including corpus analysis in methods overview courses would also be an important step forward for establishing corpus analysis in technical communication.

In arguing for classes, one must then argue for methodological resources such as textbooks, handbooks, and articles. This book covers concepts to give new researchers a starting point. Readings that further develop topics like refining questions, building and annotating a corpus, choosing an analytic contrast, deciding on units of analysis, building linguistic descriptions of the data (i.e., through collocation, keyword analysis, dispersion, etc.), recognize meaningful and non-meaningful patterns in corpus data (via significance or other means), visualizing data patterns, sampling and coding, performing intercoder reliability, conducting statistical analysis, and balancing detail and the big picture in the writing process would add to the knowledge of the nascent corpus analyst. Work on these topics exists in fields outside technical communication, but it is not tailored to the needs and topics of technical communication.

Short supplemental instruction content on corpus analysis would also be welcome. Videos of scholars explaining concepts are hugely valuable. Podcasts and other digitally-mediated ways of learning could provide targeted instruction on specific elements of corpus analysis. Seminar talks, workshops, symposia, and camps could provide instruction that is longer than a YouTube video but shorter than a semester-long class. Each of these delivery methods would aid integration of corpus tools and concepts into our research practices.

■ Research Agendas and Data Sets

Research agendas and data sets are two intertwined, critical resources for supporting technical communication corpus researchers. The boundaries of technical communication are being expanded (Carradini, 2020); research efforts are growing in social justice (Walton et al., 2019), user experience, social media (Pigg, 2020; Breuch, 2019), and emerging technologies such as virtual reality (Tham et al., 2018). As technical communication changes and expands, the field could benefit from clear attempts at agenda setting. These agendas should drive the joint development of corpus resources (e.g., corpora themselves) that could support those shared agendas. The many arms of the field ensure that no one person or even group of people can set the whole agenda for all of technical communication. Instead, researchers in each of the areas of technical communication could use corpus analysis to reflect on what previous research has uncovered and identify areas that are emerging or underrepresented. These two activities could then help researchers indicate topics of greatest need in each research area. Thus, corpus analysis can help guide researchers through reflection toward agendas for the field. In generating these resources, the field as a whole should consider the many arms of technical communication and develop agendas for where technical communication research needs to go, considering both the practitioner and scholarly ends.

Before agendas can be set in this way, corpora must be compiled and studied. There are several corpora available for analysis, such as The Technical Writing Project's corpus of student writing in technical communication (The Technical Writing Project, 2022), Purdue University's Corpus and Repository of Writing (CROW; Staples et al., 2021), University of South Florida's USF Writes, and Stephen's corpus of research abstracts in technical communication; however, more sets related to the practice of technical communication are needed.

As we have shown, building a corpus is far more difficult than collecting a bunch of stuff. A corpus requires as much care in assembly as one would give to recruiting participants for a research study. A corpus should represent a phenomenon or population that holds significance for the researchers and readers. Building a corpus takes time, resources, and perspectives that come from sharing the work with like-minded researchers. As a field of study and professional practice, we should spend time talking with each other about both the kinds of data sets that matter to us and how to build them with an eye toward making them robust and representative. The effort and energy that we put into corpus analysis ought to be aimed squarely at the priorities the field shares.

Another practical reason for focusing attention on data sets is to provide a common starting point for researchers who are studying phenomena of interest to the field. If researchers have the opportunity to work from a common data set, we have the ability to build on each other's work, consequently needing less time to advocate for the value and validity of new corpora. Short of a concerted field-wide effort to create shareable datasets, a commitment from researchers and practitioners to make sets of texts available in easily accessible ways would go a long way toward helping nascent corpus analysts get their feet wet with corpus analysis. These efforts could profitably be the focus of major professional organizations in technical communication.

■ Computing Resources and Interdisciplinary Partnerships

Anyone who has done corpus analysis will also surely point to the importance of computing resources needed to handle large corpus files. Many computers are powerful enough to handle small-to-medium sized corpora; however, some corpora are so big as to overwhelm free tools like AntConc or Lancsbox. Stephen worked with a set of Kickstarter campaigns so large (more than 320,000 texts) that his computer froze, requiring a reboot. Instead, he had to work with a collaborator who had coding skills to develop command-line tools to work with that much text. Similarly, Jason worked with corpora of several million tokens. Grinding through the data taxed the limits of his personal computer, constraining some of the analyses.

While some technical communicators and technical communication scholars will have the coding skills to design and use their own tools for corpus analysis study, many technical communication scholars (including the authors) will need collaborators with such skill. Whole volumes have been written on interdisciplinary collaboration, so we leave it at this: interdisciplinary collaborations can have high highs and low lows. Learning how to conduct these sorts of interdisciplinary collaborations effectively is a skill that will be needed for corpus analysis research to flourish in technical communication.

Another solution to the computing problem is to improve access at the institutional or organizational level. Access to high-powered computing may allow researchers to study a full corpus instead of sub-corpora, as well as greatly speed the research process. Organizations and academic institutions should consider the value of investing in computing resources capable of handling such research analysis and storing the data that the analysis is based on. This ask may be less of a problem for practitioners in large organizations and scholars in academic departments that support existing resource-hungry language analysis, such as in linguistics programs.

■ Grant Support

At the same time, professional organizations such as the Society for Technical Communication, the Association of Teachers of Technical Writing, the ACM Special Interest Group on the Design of Communication, and the Council for Programs in Scientific and Technical Communication may find it worthwhile to devote grant money for access to computing resources, whether through direct purchase or institutional access via fellowship. The grant sizes in technical communication are often small, running in the $1,000–$5,000 range. Grants to support access to computing resources could be in the $10–$20,000 (and potentially larger) range, depending on the amount of data and the cost of using the high-powered computer. Granting agencies should develop expectations about what amounts of money will be used for scraping and storage for projects of this type. Scraping and storage can often look like small tasks that don't require a lot of resources, but this is far from the truth, as anyone who has ever tried it can tell you.

■ Guidelines

Finally, technical communication practitioners and scholars need field-supported guidelines that help corpus analysis scholars conduct their work. While sets of ethical standards for internet research exist (franzke et al., 2020; Markham & Buchanan, 2012), technical communication is positioned in a distinctive space that requires different guidelines. Our field's dual focus on practitioners and scholars requires us to consider guidelines about what is ethical regarding data in the workplace being used for research, data in the wild being collected and used by researchers, and the inevitable overlaps that occur in collaboration between practitioners and researchers (Chapter 4). Developing ethical guidelines for methodological practice would be valuable for students, practitioners, and scholars alike. This effort may be undertaken in relation to other field-level initiatives, such as the *Technical Communication Body of Knowledge* (Society for Technical Communication, 2022) or one of the professional societies mentioned earlier.

Thus, we are calling upon the whole field to help develop resources for corpus analysis. These field-level resources will take much effort from many people in technical communication to develop, but these efforts are much-needed for corpus analysis to flourish in technical communication.

■ Conclusion

As awareness of corpus analysis grows in technical communication, it will become clearer how corpus analysis is a tool in the research toolbox for specific types of questions. Two types of questions stand out as meaningful for technical communication: questions of representation and change over time. Both types of questions become more meaningful as a field matures. We argued that technical communication has matured and will continue to mature in the online era, all of which makes now the right time for corpus analysis studies of what we know and how our work has changed over time.

Corpus analysis is a tool designed to answer questions that reflect on large bodies of data to determine what they represent. The field has acquired a wealth of textual outputs that reflect where the field has come from and reveal the practitioners' range of outputs. Technical communication can benefit from tools that help us understand what our work represents.

Corpus analysis can also demonstrate how corpora have changed over time. The method provides technical communication a way to respond to the shifting conditions that our practitioners and researchers find themselves in. Technical communication has always operated in this way: we develop new strategies to work with and research the conditions that develop. The topics of much technical communication work—from understanding user experience, studying issues of social justice, reviewing the effects of risk communication, planning and evaluating pedagogical experiences, developing academic programs, historicizing the discipline, characterizing the knowledge work of texts, and other research areas—can benefit from analysis that assesses how texts in those contexts have changed over time.

Ultimately, corpus analysis offers a way for technical communicators to research text at scale. Mining huge amounts of language for insights that help users, practitioners, and students is a task that will continue to be needed for the foreseeable future. We hope this book illuminates how corpus analysis is a method that can help technical communicators reflect on, extend, and expand the areas they already work in, toward ends that help people.

References

Agboka, Godwin Y. (2013). Participatory localization: A social justice approach to navigating unenfranchised/disenfranchised cultural sites. *Technical Communication Quarterly, 22*(1), 28–49. https://doi.org/10.1080/10572252.2013.730966.

Agboka, Godwin Y. (2021). "Subjects" in and of research: Decolonizing oppressive rhetorical practices in technical communication research. *Journal of Technical Writing and Communication, 51*(2), 159–174. https://doi.org/10.1177/0047281620901484.

Agostinho, Daniela, D'Ignazio, Catherine, Ring, Annie, Thylstrup, Nanna Bonde & Veel, Kristen. (2019). Uncertain archives: Approaching the unknowns, errors and vulnerabilities of big data through cultural theories of the archive. *Surveillance and Society, 17*(3/4), 422–441. https://doi.org/10.24908/ss.v17i3/4.12330.

Andersen, Rebekka. (2013). Rhetorical work in the age of content management: Implications for the field of technical communication. *Journal of Business and Technical Communication, 28*(2), 115–157. https://doi.org/10.1177/1050651913513904.

Andersen, Rebekka & Batova, Tatiana. (2015a). The current state of component content management: An integrative literature review. *IEEE Transactions on Professional Communication, 58*(3), 247–270. https://doi.org/10.1109/TPC.2016.2516619.

Andersen, Rebekka & Batova, Tatiana. (2015b). Introduction to the special issue: Content management—perspectives from the trenches. *IEEE Transactions on Professional Communication, 58*(3), 242–246. https://doi.org/10.1109/TPC.2016.2521921.

Andrews, Michael. (2020, January 11). Lumping and splitting in taxonomy. Story Needle: Content Strategy for a Post-Device Era. *WordPress.* https://storyneedle.com/lumping-and-splitting-in-taxonomy/.

Anson, Ian G., Moskovitz, Carey & Anson, Chris M. (2019). A text-analytic method for identifying text recycling in STEM research reports. *Journal of Writing Analytics, 3*(1), 125–150. https://doi.org/10.37514/JWA-J.2019.3.1.07.

Anthony, Lawrence. (2020, December 11). *AntConc* (3.5.9) [Mac/PC/Linux]. Waseda University. https://www.laurenceanthony.net/software.html

Archer, Dawn. (2009a). Does frequency really matter? In D. Archer (Ed.), *What's in a word-list? Investigating word frequency and keyword extraction* (pp. 1–16). Ashgate Publishing.

Archer, Dawn. (Ed.). (2009b). *What's in a word-list? Investigating word frequency and keyword extraction.* Ashgate Publishing.

Armaselu, Florentina. (2022). Towards a computer-assisted aesthetics of user response. *Digital Scholarship in the Humanities, 37*(1), 1–19. https://doi.org/10.1093/llc/fqab069.

Arthurs, Noah. (2018). Structural features of undergraduate writing: A computational approach. *Journal of Writing Analytics, 2*(1), 138–175. https://doi.org/10.37514/JWA-J.2018.2.1.06.

Atkins, Sue, Clear, Jeremy & Ostler, Nicholas. (1992). Corpus design criteria. *Literary and Linguistic Computing, 7*(1), 1–16. https://doi.org/10.1093/llc/7.1.1.

Aull, Laura. (2017). Corpus analysis of argumentative versus explanatory discourse in writing task genres. *Journal of Writing Analytics, 1*(1), 1–47. https://doi.org/10.37514/JWA-J.2017.1.1.03.

Aull, Laura L. & Lancaster, Zak. (2014). Linguistic markers of stance in early and advanced academic writing: A corpus-based comparison. *Written Communication, 31*(2), 151–183. https://doi.org/10.1177/0741088314527055.

Austin, John L. (1962). *How to do things with words.* Oxford University Press.

Baek, Seung-ji, Jeong, Hayeong & Kobayashi, Kyoshi. (2013). Disaster anxiety measurement and corpus-based content analysis of crisis communication. In H. Krautwurmová (Ed.), *2013 IEEE International Conference on Systems, Man, and Cybernetics* (pp. 1789–1794). https://doi.org/10.1109/SMC.2013.309.

Baker, Mark. (2013). *Every page is page one: Topic-based writing for technical communication and the web.* XML Press.

Baker, Paul. (2006). *Using corpora in discourse analysis.* Continuum.

Baker, Paul. (2012). *Contemporary corpus linguistics.* Bloomsbury.

Bakhtin, Mikhail M. (1981). *The dialogic imagination: Four essays* (M. Holquist, Ed.; C. Emerson, Trans.; Revised edited edition). University of Texas Press.

Baroni, Marco & Bernardini, Silvia. (2004). BootCaT: Bootstrapping corpora and terms from the web. In M. T. Lino, M. F. Xavier, F. Ferreira, R. Costa & R. Silva (Eds.), *Proceedings of the Fourth International Conference on Language Resources and Evaluation.* http://www.lrec-conf.org/proceedings/lrec2004/pdf/509.pdf.

Barton, Ellen. L. (1993). Evidentials, argumentation, and epistemological stance. *College English, 55*(7), 745–769. https://doi.org/10.2307/378428.

Barton, Ellen. (2004). Discourse methods and critical practice in professional communication: The front-stage and back-stage discourse of prognosis in medicine. *Journal of Business and Technical Communication, 18*(1), 67–111. https://doi.org/10.1177/105065 1903258127.

Barton, Ellen, Thominet, Luke, Boeder, Ruth & Primeau, Sarah. (2018). Do community members have an effective voice in the ethical deliberation of a behavioral institutional review board? *Journal of Business and Technical Communication, 32*(2), 154–197. https://doi.org/10.1177/1050651917746460.

Bellamy, Laura, Carey, Michelle & Schlotfeldt, Jenifer. (2012). *DITA best practices: A roadmap for writing, editing, and architecting in DITA.* IBM Press.

Berberich, Kristin & Kleiber, Ingo. (2023). Corpus-analysis.com.

Biber, Douglas. (1993). Representativeness in corpus design. *Literary and Linguistic Computing, 8*(4), 243–257. https://doi.org/10.1093/llc/8.4.243.

Biber, Douglas, Conrad, Susan & Reppen, Randi. (2000). *Corpus linguistics: Investigating language structure and use.* Cambridge University Press.

Boettger, Ryan K. & Friess, Erin. (2016). Academics are from Mars, practitioners are from Venus: Analyzing content alignment within technical communication forums. *Technical Communication, 63*(4), 314–327.

Boettger, Ryan K. & Ishizaki, Suguru. (2018). Introduction to the special issue: data-driven approaches to research and teaching in professional and technical communication. *IEEE Transactions on Professional Communication, 61*(4), 352-355. https://doi .org/10.1109/TPC.2018.2870547.

Boettger, Ryan K. & Wulff, Stephanie. (2014). The naked truth about the naked this: Investigating grammatical prescriptivism in technical communication. *Technical Communication Quarterly, 23*(2), 115-140. https://doi.org/10.1080/10572252.2013.803919.

Boettger, Ryan K. & Wulff, Stephanie. (2022). *The Technical Writing Project.* WordPress. http://technicalwritingproject.com/.

Breuch, Lee-Ann Kastman. (2019). *Involving the audience: A rhetorical perspective on using social media to improve websites*. Routledge/Taylor & Francis Group.

Brezina, Vaclav. (2018). *Statistics in corpus linguistics: A practical guide*. Cambridge University Press.

Brezina, Vaclav, Weill-Tessier, Pierre & McEnery, Anthony. (2020). *#LancsBox: Lancaster University corpus toolbox* (v. 5.x) [Computer software]. http://corpora.lancs.ac.uk /lancsbox.

Brooker, Phillip, Barnett, Julie & Cribbin, Timothy. (2016). Doing social media analytics. *Big Data & Society, 3*(2), 1–12. https://doi.org/10.1177/2053951716658060.

Brown, Gillian & Yule, George. (1983). *Discourse analysis*. Cambridge University Press.

Brumberger, Eva & Lauer, Claire. (2015). The evolution of technical communication: An analysis of industry job postings. *Technical Communication, 62*(4), 224–243.

Campbell, Kim S., Naidoo, Jefrey S. & Campbell, Sean M. (2020). Hard or soft sell? Understanding white papers as content marketing. *IEEE Transactions on Professional Communication, 63*(1), 21–38. https://doi.org/10.1109/TPC.2019.2961000.

Carradini, Stephen. (2020). A comparison of research topics associated with technical communication, business communication, and professional communication, 1963–2017. *IEEE Transactions on Professional Communication, 63*(2), 118–138. https://doi.org /10.1109/TPC.2020.2988757.

Carradini, Stephen. (2022). The ship of Theseus: Change over time in topics of technical communication research abstracts. In J. Schreiber & L. Melonçon (Eds.), *Assembling critical components: A framework for sustaining technical and professional communication* (pp. 39–68). https://doi.org/10.37514/tpc-b.2022.1381.2.02.

Carradini, S. & Fleischmann, C. (2023). The effects of multimodal elements on success in Kickstarter crowdfunding campaigns. *Journal of Business and Technical Communication, 37*(1), 1-27. https://doi.org/10.1177/1050651922121699.

Carroll, John M. (1990). *The Nurnberg funnel: Designing minimalist instruction for practical computer skill*. The MIT Press.

Charmaz, Kathy. (2014). *Constructing grounded theory* (2nd ed.). SAGE Publications.

Connor, Jennifer J. (1993). Medical text and historical context: Research issues and methods in history and technical communication. *Journal of Technical Writing and Communication, 23*(3), 211-232. https://doi.org/10.2190/0p4q-07x0-r2ev-wrd2.

Connors, Robert J. (1982). The rise of writing instruction in America. *Journal of Technical Writing and Communication, 12*(4), 329-352. https://doi.org/10.1177/00472816820 1200406.

Conrad, Susan. (2017). The use of passives and impersonal style in civil engineering writing. *Journal of Business and Technical Communication, 32*(1), 38-76. https://doi.org/10 .1177/1050651917729864.

Corpus of Contemporary American English (COCA). (n.d.). Retrieved January 15, 2021, from https://www.english-corpora.org/coca/.

Corrigan, Julie A. & Slomp, David H. (2021). Articulating a sociocognitive construct of writing expertise for the digital age. *Journal of Writing Analytics, 5*(1), 142–195. https:// doi.org/10.37514/JWA-J.2021.5.1.05.

Crawford, William J. & Csomay, Eniko. (2016). *Doing corpus linguistics*. Routledge.

Creswell, John W. (1994). *Research design: Qualitative and quantitative approaches*. Sage.

Cross, Cate & Oppenheim, Charles. (2006). A genre analysis of scientific abstracts. *Journal of Documentation, 62*(4), 428–446. https://doi.org/10.1108/00220410610700953.

Dryer, Dylan B. (2013). Scaling writing ability: A corpus-driven inquiry. *Written Communication, 30*(1), 3–35. https://doi.org/10.1177/0741088312466992.

Dryer, Dylan B. (2019). Divided by primes: Competing meanings among writing studies' keywords. *College English, 81*(3), 214–255.

Durack, Katherine T. (1997). Gender, technology, and the history of technical communication. *Technical Communication Quarterly, 6*(3), 249–260. https://doi.org/10.1207/s15427625tcq0603_2.

Dushnitsky, Gary & Fitza, Markus A. (2018). Are we missing the platforms for the crowd? Comparing investment drivers across multiple crowdfunding platforms. *Journal of Business Venturing Insights, 10*. e00100. https://doi.org/10.1016/j.jbvi.2018.e00100.

Eble, Michelle F. (2003). Content vs. product: The effects of single sourcing on the teaching of technical communication. *Technical Communication, 50*(3), 344–349.

Education First. (2021). *Infinitive.* https://www.ef.edu/english-resources/english-grammar/infinitive/.

Egbert, Jesse. (2019). Corpus design and representativeness. In T. B. Sardinha & M. V. Pinto (Eds.), *Multi-dimensional analysis: Research methods and current issues* (pp. 27–42). Bloomsbury Publishing.

Erickson, Lief. (2019). *The role of taxonomy and search in content usability* [Master's thesis, FH Joanneum]. https://epub.fh-joanneum.at/obvfhjhs/content/titleinfo/4403250/full.pdf.

Evia, Carlos. (2018). *Creating intelligent content with lightweight DITA.* Routledge.

Fahnestock, Jeanne. (1986). Accommodating science: The rhetorical life of scientific facts. *Written Communication, 3*(3), 275–296. https://doi.org/10.1177/0741088386003003001.

Flanagan, Suzan. (2015). Intelligent content editing: A prototype theory for managing digital content. *International Journal of Sociotechnology and Knowledge Development, 7*(4), 53–57. https://doi.org/10.4018/IJSKD.2015100104.

Fletcher, William. H. (2007). Concordancing the web: Promise and problems, tools and techniques. In M. Hundt, N. Nesselhauf & C. Biewer (Eds.), *Corpus linguistics and the web* (pp. 25–45). Brill Rodopi.

franzke, aline shakti, Bechmann, Anja, Zimmer, Michael, Ess, Charles M. & the Association of Internet Researchers. (2020). Internet research: Ethical guidelines 3.0. https://aoir.org/reports/ethics3.pdf.

Gablasova, Dana, Brezina, Vaclav & McEnery, Tony. (2019). The Trinity Lancaster Corpus: Development, description and application. *International Journal of Learner Corpus Research, 5*(2), 126–158.

Gallagher, John R., Chen, Yinyin, Wagner, Kyle, Wang, Xuan, Zeng, Jingyi & Kong, Alyssa Lingyi. (2020). Peering into the internet abyss: Using big data audience analysis to understand online comments. *Technical Communication Quarterly, 29*(2), 155–173. https://doi.org/10.1080/10572252.2019.1634766.

Garside, Roger, Fligelstone, Steve & Botley, Simon. (2013). Discourse annotation: Anaphoric relations in corpora. In R. Garside, G. Leech & T. McEnery (Eds.), *Corpus annotation: Linguistic information from computer text corpora* (pp. 66–84). Routledge.

Garside, Roger, Leech, Geoffrey & McEnery, Tony (Eds.). (2013). *Corpus annotation: Linguistic information from computer text corpora.* Routledge.

Gee, James P. (2005). *An introduction to discourse analysis: Theory and method* (2nd ed.). Routledge.

Geisler, Cheryl & Swarts, Jason. (2019). *Coding streams of language: Techniques for the systematic coding of text, talk, and other verbal data.* The WAC Clearinghouse; University Press of Colorado. https://doi.org/10.37514/PRA-B.2019.0230.

Gerbig, Andrea. (2010). Key words and key phrases in a corpus of travel writing: From early modern English literature to contemporary "blooks." In M. Bondi & M. Scott (Eds.), *Keyness in texts* (pp. 147–168). John Benjamins Publishing.

Gibson, J. J. (1986). *The ecological approach to visual perception.* Lawrence Erlbaum Associates.

Gillespie, Rob. (2017, January 5). *DITA and topic-based writing: Flip sides of the same coin? CIDM.* LinkedIn.file:///Users/jswarts/Downloads https://www.linkedin.com/pulse/dita-topic-based-writing-flip-sides-same-coin-rob-gillespie/.

Glaser, Barney G. (1965). The constant comparative method of qualitative analysis. *Social Problems, 12*(4), 436–445. https://doi.org/10.2307/798843

Glaser, Barney & Strauss, Anselm. (1967). *The discovery of grounded theory.* Aldine Publishing.

Goffman, Erving. (1974). *Frame analysis: An essay on the organization of experience.* Harvard University Press.

Goody, Jack & Watt, Ian. (1963). The consequences of literacy. *Comparative Studies in Society and History, 5*(3), 304–345. https://doi.org/10.1017/S0010417500001730.

Graham, S. Scott, Kim, Sang-Yeon, DeVasto, Danielle M. & Keith, William. (2015). Statistical genre analysis: Toward big data methodologies in technical communication. *Technical Communication Quarterly, 24*(1), 70–104. https://doi.org/10.1080/105722 52.2015.975955.

Hackos, JoAnn T. & IBM. (2006). *What is topic-based authoring?* [Concept]. http://dita-ot.sourceforge.net/doc/ot-userguide13/xhtml/faqs/topic_authoring.html.

Hackos, JoAnn T. (2002). *Content management for dynamic web delivery.* John Wiley & Sons.

Halliday, M. A. K. (2004). *An introduction to functional grammar* (3rd ed.). Arnold Publishers.

Halvorson, Kristina & Rach, Melissa. (2012). *Content strategy for the web.* New Riders.

Hardie, Andrew. (2014). *Log ratio—an informal introduction.* ESRC Centre for Corpus Approaches to Social Science (CASS). http://cass.lancs.ac.uk/log-ratio-an-informal-introduction/.

Harré, Rom. (2002). Material objects in social worlds. *Theory, Culture & Society, 19*(5–6), 23–33. https://doi.org/10.1177/026327640201900502.

Henry, Alex & Roseberry, Robert L. (2001). A narrow-angled corpus analysis of moves and strategies of the genre: "Letter of Application." *English for Specific Purposes, 20*(2), 153–167. https://doi.org/10.1016/S0889-4906(99)00037-X.

Heritage, John. (2012). Epistemics in conversation. In J. Sidnell & T. Stivers (Eds.), *The Handbook of Conversation Analysis* (pp. 370–394). John Wiley & Sons. https://doi.org/10.1002/9781118325001.ch18.

hiQ Labs, Inc. v. LinkedIn Corp. 273 F. Supp. 3d 1099, 1103 (N.D. Cal. 2019).

Hodges, Amy & Seawright, Leslie. (2019). Writing in transnational workplaces: Teaching strategies for multilingual engineers. *IEEE Transactions on Professional Communication, 62*(3), 298–309. https://doi.org/10.1109/TPC.2019.2930178.

Holcomb, Chris & Buell, Duncan A. (2018). First-year composition as "big data": Towards examining student revisions at scale. *Computers and Composition, 48*, 49–66. https://doi.org/10.1016/j.compcom.2018.03.003.

Horn, Robert E., Nicol, Elizabeth H., Kleinman, Joel C. & Grace, Michael G. (1969). *Information mapping for learning and reference*. Information Resources.

Hyland, Ken. (2005). *Metadiscourse: Exploring interaction in writing*. Continuum.

Ishizaki, Suguru. (2016). Computer-aided rhetorical analysis of crowdfunding pitches. In E. Friess & C. Lam (Eds.), *2016 IEEE International Professional Communication Conference (IPCC)* (pp. 1–4). https://doi.org/10.1109/IPCC.2016.7740540.

Itchuaqiyaq, Cana Uluak & Matheson, Breeanne. (2021). Decolonizing decoloniality: Considering the (mis) use of decolonial frameworks in TPC scholarship. *Communication Design Quarterly, 9*(1), 20–31. https://doi.org/10.1145/3437000.3437002.

Johnson, Tom. (2020, March 30). *Are technical writers increasingly playing non-technical roles? Some thoughts on the evolution of technical writing roles*. I'd Rather Be Writing. https://idratherbewriting.com/blog/evolving-roles-of-technical-wrters/.

Johnstone, Barbara. (2017). *Discourse analysis*. John Wiley & Sons.

Kaptelinin, Victor. (1996). Computer-mediated activity: Functional organs in social and developmental contexts. In B. A. Nardi (Ed.), *Context and consciousness: Activity theory and human-computer interaction* (pp. 45–68). MIT Press.

Karatsolis, Andreas. (2016). Rhetorical patterns in citations across disciplines and levels of participation. *Journal of Writing Research, 7*(3), 425–452. https://doi.org/10.17239/jowr-2016.07.03.06.

Kaufer, David & Ishizaki, Suguru. (1998). *DocuScope: Computer-aided rhetorical analysis*. Carnegie Mellon. https://www.cmu.edu/dietrich/english/research-and-publications/docuscope.html.

Kaufer, David & Ishizaki, Suguru. (2006). A corpus study of canned letters: Mining the latent rhetorical proficiencies marketed to writers-in-a-hurry and non-writers. *IEEE Transactions on Professional Communication, 49*(3), 254–266. https://doi.org/10.1109/TPC.2006.880743

Kaufer, David, Ishizaki, Sugu.ru & Cai, Xizhen. (2016). Analyzing the language of citation across discipline and experience levels: An automated dictionary approach. *Journal of Writing Research, 7*(3), 453–483. https://doi.org/10.17239/jowr-2016.07.03.07.

Kennedy, Graeme D. (2014). *An introduction to corpus linguistics*. Routledge.

Kim, Dave & Olson, Wendy M. (2020). Using a transfer-focused writing pedagogy to improve undergraduates' lab report writing in gateway engineering laboratory courses. *IEEE Transactions on Professional Communication, 63*(1), 64–84. https://doi.org/10.1109/TPC.2019.2961009.

Koene, Ansgar, Adolphs, Svenja, Perez, Elvira, Carter, Christopher, Statache, Ramona, O'Malley, Claire, Rodden, Tom & McAuley, Derek. (2015). Ethics considerations for corpus linguistic studies using internet resources. In In F. Formato & A. Hardie (Eds.), *Corpus Linguistics* (pp. 204–206). Lancaster University.

Kohl, John R. (2008). *The global English style guide: Writing clear, translatable documentation for a global market*. SAS Institute.

Krippendorff, Klaus. (2018). *Content analysis: An introduction to its methodology* (4th ed.). SAGE Publications.

Krull, Robert. (1997). What practitioners need to know to evaluate research. *IEEE Transactions on Professional Communication, 40*(3), 168–181. https://doi.org/10.1109/47.649553.

Kuebler, Sandra & Zinsmeister, Heike. (2015). *Corpus linguistics and linguistically annotated corpora*. Bloomsbury Publishing.

Kynell, Teresa. (1999) Technical communication from 1850–1950: Where have we been?, *Technical Communication Quarterly, 8*(2), 143–151. https://doi.org/10.1080/10572259909364655

Lam, Phoenix W. (2013). Interdiscursivity, hypertextuality, multimodality: A corpus-based multimodal move analysis of internet group buying deals. *Journal of Pragmatics, 51*, 13–39. https://doi.org/10.1016/j.pragma.2013.02.006.

Lane, Charles. (2017, March 31). *Will using artificial intelligence to make loans trade one kind of bias for another?* NPR. https://www.npr.org/sections/alltechconsidered/2017/03/31/521946210/will-using-artificial-intelligence-to-make-loans-trade-one-kind-of-bias-for-anot.

Latour, Bruno & Woolgar, Steve. (1979). *Laboratory life: The social construction of scientific facts.* Sage.

Lauer, Janice M. & Asher, J. William. (1988). *Composition research: Empirical designs.* Oxford University Press.

Lauren, Benjamin & Schreiber, Joanna. (2018). An integrative literature review of project management in technical and professional communication. *Technical Communication, 65*(1), 85–106.

Laursen, Anne Lise, Mousten, Birthe, Jensen, Vigdis & Kampf, Constance. (2014). Using an AD-HOC corpus to write about emerging technologies for technical writing and translation: The case of search engine optimization. *IEEE Transactions on Professional Communication, 57*(1), 56–74. https://doi.org/10.1109/TPC.2014.2307011.

Leech, Geoffrey. (2004). Adding linguistic annotation. In M. Wynne (Ed.), *Developing linguistic corpora: A guide to good practice.* ahds: literature, language and linguistics. http://users.ox.ac.uk/~martinw/dlc/chapter2.htm.

Leech, Geoffrey. (2007). New resources, or just better old ones? The Holy Grail of representativeness. In M. Hundt, N. Nesselhauf & C. Biewer (Eds.), *Corpus linguistics and the web* (pp. 133–149). Brill Rodopi.

Leech, Geoffrey. (2013). Introducing corpus annotation. In R. Garside, G. Leech & T. McEnery (Eds.), *Corpus annotation: Linguistic information from computer text corpora* (pp. 1–18). Routledge.

Leech, Geoffrey, McEnery, Tony & Wynne, Martin. (2013). Further levels of annotation. In R. Garside, G. Leech & T. McEnery (Eds.), *Corpus annotation: Linguistic information from computer text corpora* (pp. 85–101). Routledge.

Leijen, Djuddah A. (2017). A novel approach to examine the impact of web-based peer review on the revisions of L2 writers. *Computers and Composition, 43*, 35–54. https://doi.org/10.1016/j.compcom.2016.11.005.

Lüdeling, Anke, Evert, Stefan & Baroni, Marco. (2007). Using web data for linguistic purposes. In M. Hundt, N. Nesselhauf & C. Biewer (Eds.), *Corpus linguistics and the web* (pp. 7–24). Brill Rodopi.

Mackiewicz, Jo & Thompson, Isabelle K. (2015). *Talk about writing: The tutoring strategies of experienced writing center tutors.* Routledge.

Malone, Edward A. (2007). Historical studies of technical communication in the United States and England: A fifteen-year retrospection and guide to resources. *IEEE Transactions on Professional Communication, 50*(4), 333–351. http://doi.org/10.1109/TPC.2007.908732.

Markham, Annette & Buchanan, Elizabeth. (2012). *Ethical decision-making and internet research: Version 2.0.* Association of Internet Researchers. http://www.uwstout.edu/ethicscenter/upload/aoirethicsprintablecopy.pdf.

McLuhan, Marshall. (1994). *Understanding media: The extensions of man.* MIT Press.

Mehlenbacher, Ashley Rose. (2019). Registered reports: Genre evolution and the research article. *Written Communication, 36*(1), 38–67. https://doi.org/10.1177/0741088 318804534.

Melonçon, Lisa. (2012). The rise of academic programs: A call for collaboration. *Intercom, 59*(7), 13–15.

Miller, Bridget. (2019, June 4). *Pros of using AI in the recruiting process.* HR Daily Advisor. https://hrdailyadvisor.blr.com/2019/06/04/pros-of-using-ai-in-the-recruiting -process/.

Miller, Benjamin & Licastro, Amanda. (2021). Introduction: Reasons to engage composition through big data. In A. Licastro & B. Miller (Eds.), *Composition and Big Data* (pp. 3–21). University of Pittsburgh Press.

Miller, Carolyn. R. (1984). Genre as social action. *Quarterly Journal of Speech, 70*(2), 151–167. https://doi.org/10.1080/00335638409383686.

Miller, Carolyn R., Devitt, Amy J. & Gallagher, Victoria J. (2018). Genre: Permanence and change. *Rhetoric Society Quarterly, 48*(3), 269–277. https://doi.org/10.1080/0277394 5.2018.1454194.

Mueller, Derek N. (2019). *Network sense: Methods for visualizing a discipline.* The WAC Clearinghouse; University Press of Colorado. https://doi.org/10.37514/WRI-B.2017 .0124.

Noble, Safiya U. (2018). *Algorithms of oppression: How Search Engines Reinforce Racism.* New York University Press.

Norman, Donald. (1989). *The design of everyday things.* Basic Books.

Oakes, Michael P. (1998/2019). *Statistics for corpus linguistics.* Edinburgh University Press.

Omizo, Ryan & Hart-Davidson, William. (2016a). Hedge-O-Matic. *Enculturation, 7.* http://hedgeomatic.cal.msu.edu/hedgeomatic/.

Omizo, Ryan & Hart-Davidson, William. (2016b). Finding genre signals in academic writing. *Journal of Writing Research, 7*(3), 485–509. https://doi.org/10.17239/jowr-2016 .07.03.08.

O'Neil, Cathy. (2016). *Weapons of math destruction: How big data increases inequality and threatens democracy.* Crown.

O'Neil, Fer. (2015). Perceptions of content authoring methodologies in technical communication: The perceived benefits of single sourcing. *2015 IEEE International Professional Communication Conference (IPCC)* (pp. 1–8). https://doi.org/10.1109 /IPCC.2015.7235840.

Ong, Walter J. (2018). *Language as hermeneutic: A primer on the word and digitization.* Cornell University Press.

Orr, Thomas. (2006). Introduction to the special issue: Insights from corpus linguistics for professional communication. *IEEE Transactions on Professional Communication, 49*(3), 213–216. https://doi.org/10.1109/TPC.2006.880750.

Paradis, James. (1991). Text and action: The operator's manual in context and in court. In C. Bazerman & J. Paradis (Eds.), *Textual dynamics of the professions: Historical and contemporary studies of writing in professional communities* (pp. 256–278). University of Wisconsin Press.

Peele, Thomas. (2018). Is this too polite? The limited use of rhetorical moves in a first-year corpus. *Journal of Writing Analytics, 2*(1), 78–95. https://doi.org/10.37514/JWA -J.2018.2.1.04.

Pennebaker, James W. (2011). *The secret life of pronouns: What our words say about us.* Bloomsbury Press.

Petersen, Emily January & Walton, Rebecca. (2018). Bridging analysis and action: How feminist scholarship can inform the social justice turn. *Journal of Business and Technical Communication, 32*(4), 416–446. https://doi.org/10.1177/1050651918780192.

Pflugfelder, Ehren Helmut. (2017). Reddit's "Explain Like I'm Five": Technical descriptions in the wild. *Technical Communication Quarterly, 26*(1), 25–41. https://doi.org/10.1080/10572252.2016.1257741.

Pigg, Stacey. (2020). *Transient literacies in action: Composing with the mobile surround.* The WAC Clearinghouse; University Press of Colorado. https://doi.org/10.37514/WRI-B.2020.1015.

Pirolli, Peter. (2007). *Information foraging theory: Adaptive interaction with information.* Oxford University Press.

Pirolli, Peter & Card, Stuart. (1995). Information foraging in information access environments. In I. R. Katz, R. Mack, L. Marks, M. B. Rosson & J. Nielsen (Eds.), *Proceedings of the SIGCHI Conference on Human Factors in Computing Systems* (pp. 51–58). https://doi.org/10.1145/223904.223911.

Priestley, Michael, Hargis, Gretchen & Carpenter, Susan. (2001). DITA: An XML-based technical documentation authoring and publishing architecture. *Technical Communication, 48*(3), 352–367.

Rayson, Paul. (n.d.). Free USAS English web tagger. https://ucrel-api.lancaster.ac.uk/usas/tagger.hrml.

Redish, Janice C. (1989). Reading to learn to do. *IEEE Transactions on Professional Communication, 32*(4), 289–293. https://doi.org/10.1109/47.44542.

Redish, Janice C. (1993). Understanding readers. In C. M. Barnum & S. Carliner (Eds.), *Techniques for technical communicators* (pp. 15–41). Macmillan.

Reppen, Randi. (2010). Building a corpus. In M. J. McCarthy & A. O'Keefe (Eds.), *The Routledge handbook of corpus linguistics* (pp. 31–37). Routledge.

Robles, Vincent D. (2018). Resolving discourse at technical-support helpdesks. *IEEE Transactions on Professional Communication, 61*(3), 275–294. https://doi.org/10.1109/TPC.2018.2813178.

Rockley, Ann, Manning, Steve & Cooper, Charles. (2009). *DITA 101: Fundamentals of DITA for authors and managers.* The Rockley Group.

Rorty, Richard. (1979). *Philosophy and the mirror of nature.* Princeton University Press.

Rude, Carolyn D. (1995). The report for decision making: Genre and inquiry. *Journal of Business and Technical Communication, 9*(2), 170–205. https://doi.org/10.1177/1050651995009002002.

Rude, Carolyn D. (2009). Mapping the research questions in technical communication. *Journal of Business and Technical Communication, 23*(2), 174–215. https://doi.org/10.1177/1050651908329562.

Saldaña, Johnny. (2016). *The coding manual for qualitative researchers* (3rd ed.). Sage.

Sanders, Ted J., Spooren, Wilbert P. & Noordman, Leo G. (1992). Toward a taxonomy of coherence relations. *Discourse Processes, 15*(1), 1–35. http://dx.doi.org/10.1080/01638539209544800.

Sapienza, Filipp. (2007). A rhetorical approach to single-sourcing via intertextuality. *Technical Communication Quarterly, 16*(1), 83–101. https://doi.org/10.1080/10572250709336578.

Scott, Mike. (1997). PC analysis of key words—And key key words. *System, 25*(2), 233–245. https://doi.org/10.1016/S0346-251X(97)00011-0.

Scott, Mike. (2009). In search of a bad reference corpus. In D. Archer (Ed.), *What's in a Word-list?* (pp. 79–92). Ashgate.

Searle, John R. (1985). *Expression and meaning: Studies in the theory of speech acts.* Cambridge University Press.

Shelton, Cecilia. (2020). Shifting out of neutral: Centering difference, bias, and social justice in a business writing course. *Technical Communication Quarterly, 29*(1), 18–32. https://doi.org/10.1080/10572252.2019.1640287.

Smith, Jordan. (2022). Corpus linguistics and technical editing: How corpora can help copy editors adopt a rhetorical view of prescriptive usage rules. *Journal of Business and Technical Communication.* https://doi.org/10.1177/10506519221143125.

Society for Technical Communication. (n.d.). *About STC.* https://www.stc.org/about-stc/.

Society for Technical Communication. (2022). *About the Technical Communication Body of Knowledge.* https://www.tcbok.org/

Sonnenberg, Michelle, Gubala, Carolyn, Burry, Justiss, Griffith, Jessica, Zarlengo, Tanya & Melonçon, Lisa. (2022). Implementing a continuous improvement model for assignment evaluation at the technical and professional communication program level. *Journal of Technical Writing and Communication.* https://doi.org/10.1177/00472816221124605.

Spartz, John M. & Weber, Ryan P. (2015). Writing entrepreneurs: A survey of attitudes, habits, skills, and genres. *Journal of Business and Technical Communication, 29*(4), 428–455.

Spinuzzi, Clay. (2003). *Tracing genres through organizations: A sociocultural approach to information design.* MIT Press.

Spinuzzi, Clay, Nelson, Scott, Thomson, Keela S., Lorenzini, Francesca, French, Rosemary A., Pogue, Gregory, Burback, Sidney D. & Momberger, Joel. (2014). Making the pitch: Examining dialogue and revisions in entrepreneurs' pitch decks. *IEEE Transactions on Professional Communication, 57*(3), 158–181. https://doi.org/10.1109/TPC.2014.2342354.

Spyridakis, Jan H. (1989). Signaling effects: Increased content retention and new answers—Part II. *Journal of Technical Writing and Communication, 19*(4), 395–415. https://doi.org/10.2190/493Q-703B-JBVD-E0T9.

Staples, Shelly, Picoral, Adriana, Macdonald, Lindsey, Gao, Jie & Wang, Zhaozhe. (2021). *Crow.* Corpus & Repository of Writing. https://writecrow.org/

Stephens, Eric. (2018). *Prisons, genres, and big data: Understanding the language of corrections in America's prisons* [Doctoral dissertation, Clemson University]. https://tigerprints.clemson.edu/all_dissertations/2103.

Suchman, Lucy A. (2007). *Human-machine reconfigurations: Plans and situated actions.* Cambridge University Press.

Swales, John M. (1990). *Genre analysis: English in academic and research settings.* Cambridge University Press.

Swales, John M. (2011). *Aspects of article introductions.* University of Michigan Press.

Swarts, Jason. (2018). *Wicked, incomplete, and uncertain: User support in the wild and the role of technical communication.* Utah State University Press.

Swarts, Jason. (2022). Uses of metadiscourse in online help. *Written Communication, 39*(4), 689–721. https://doi.org/10.1177/07410883221109241.

Tardy, Christine M., Sommer-Farias, Bruna & Gevers, Jeroen. (2020). Teaching and researching genre knowledge: Toward an enhanced theoretical framework. *Written Communication, 37*(3), 287–321. https://doi.org/10.1177/0741088320916554.

Tashea, Jason. (2017, April 17). Courts are using AI to sentence criminals. That must stop now. *Wired.* https://www.wired.com/2017/04/courts-using-ai-sentence-criminals -must-stop-now/.

Tham, Jason, Duin, Ann Hill, Gee, Laura, Ernst, Nathan, Abdelqader, Bilal & McGrath, Megan. (2018). Understanding virtual reality: Presence, embodiment, and professional practice. *IEEE Transactions on Professional Communication, 61*(2), 178–195. https:// doi.org/10.1109/TPC.2018.2804238.

Thralls, Charlotte & Blyler, Nancy Roundy. (1993). The social perspective and pedagogy in technical communication. *Technical Communication Quarterly, 2*(3), 249–270. https://doi.org/10.1080/10572259309364540.

Turner, Heather Noel. (2022). Key-notes: A Content Analysis of ATTW Conferences 1998–2018. *Technical Communication Quarterly, 31*(4), 401–415. https://doi.org/10.1080 /10572252.2022.2034975.

Upton, Thomas A. & Cohen, Mary Ann. (2009). An approach to corpus-based discourse analysis: The move analysis as example. *Discourse Studies, 11*(5), 585–605. https://doi .org/10.1177/1461445609341006.

University of South Florida. (2023). *Department of English; USF Writes; FAQs.* https:// www.usf.edu/arts-sciences/departments/english/writing-programs/usf-writes-faq.aspx.

Walczak, Steven. (2017). A text analytic approach to classifying document types. *Journal of Writing Analytics, 1*(1), 103–146. https://doi.org/10.37514/JWA-J.2017.1.1.06.

Walton, R., Moore, Kristen R. & Jones, Natasha N. (2019). *Technical communication after the social justice turn: Building coalitions for action.* Routledge.

Weedon, J. Scott. (2020). Emotion and the economy of genre in a design presentation. *Technical Communication Quarterly, 29*(2), 188–201. https://doi.org/10.1080/10572252.2 019.1689297.

Wenger, Etienne. (1998). *Communities of practice: Learning, meaning and identity.* Cambridge University Press.

Wetzel, Danielle, Brown, David, Werner, Necia, Ishizaki, Suguru & Kaufer, David. (2021). Computer-assisted rhetorical analysis: Instructional design and formative assessment using DocuScope. *Journal of Writing Analytics, 5*(1), 292–323. https://doi .org/10.37514/JWA-J.2021.5.1.09.

White, Kate, Rumsey, Suzanne Kesler & Amidon, Stevens. (2015). Are we "there" yet? The treatment of gender and feminism in technical, business, and workplace writing studies. *Journal of Technical Writing and Communication, 46*(1), 27–58. https://doi.org /10.1177/0047281615600637.

Williams, Joseph M. (1997). *Style: Ten lessons in clarity and grace* (5th ed.). Addison Wesley.

Wilson, Andrew & Thomas, Jenny. (2013). Semantic annotation. In R. Garside, G. Leech & T. McEnery (Eds.), *Corpus annotation: Linguistic information from computer text corpora* (pp. 53–65). Routledge.

Wolfe, Joanna. (2009). How technical communication textbooks fail engineering students. *Technical Communication Quarterly, 18*(4), 351–375. https://doi.org/10.1080 /10572250903149662.

Yates, JoAnne. (1993). *Control through communication: The rise of system in American management.* The Johns Hopkins University Press.

Zanchetta, Eros, Baroni, Marco & Bernardini, Silvia. (2011, July 20–22). *Corpora for the masses: The BootCaT front end* [Paper presentation.] Corpus Linguistics Conference, International Convention Centre (ICC), Birmingham, UK.

Zhang, Jiajie & Patel, Vimla L. (2006). Distributed cognition, representation, and affordance. *Pragmatics & Cognition, 14*(2), 333–341. https://doi.org/10.1075/pc.14.2.12zha.

Glossary

Aboutness: a reader's perception of a text's or corpus' overall meaning or focus, separate from—but often reinforced by—the presence of keywords.

Annotation: a process of adding information to the language content of a text or corpus. Annotations may be "representational" in that they describe text (e.g., orthographic annotation, such as marking the beginning and ending of words) or "interpretive" in that they add analysis to text (e.g., pragmatic annotation, such as describing how language is used).

Balancedness: a characteristic of corpus design and creation referring to the intentional and proportional representation of all forms of language content that a corpus is meant to represent.

Collocation: a) an analytic process based on finding two or more words or phrases that occur near each other within texts in a corpus. Such words or phrases are said to be "co-located" or "collocates." b) a tool built into corpus analysis software that is capable of counting the actual and expected frequency of word or phrase co-location.

Concordance: a) a listing of every instance of a word or phrase appearing in a corpus of texts; b) a tool built into corpus analysis software that is capable of locating and listing every instance of a word or phrase appearing in a corpus of texts.

Concordance lines: a listing of every instance of a word or phrase in a corpus, including the words to the left and right which make up the word's or phrase's context.

Corpora: plural form of "corpus," referring to more than one collection of texts used in analysis. Often used when comparing two collections of text in one analysis.

Corpus: a collection of texts that share a common trait, source, subject, form, or function. The collection is usually a sample of texts that represent the larger population of texts from which they are drawn. Examples might include white papers on an emerging technology, op-eds on education, or presidential speeches.

Dictionary: a) a collection of words or phrases organized into groups that represent a shared characteristic or meaning (e.g., action verbs, hedges, negative evaluation words, evidentials); b) a resource used in computer-assisted content analysis to automate coding of that content by matching words or phrases in a corpus with a collection of other words organized in the way described in definition a.

Discourse: a) a stream of written or spoken words usually exchanged between speakers or correspondents; b) broadly, any form of intentional communication, whether between co-present participants or those who are not co-present (e.g., a writer and reader).

Dispersion: a measure of the degree to which a word or phrase is spread through texts that comprise the corpus. A high dispersion score indicates that a word or phrase appears in many texts in a corpus. A low dispersion score indicates more sporadic spread of a word or phrase throughout a corpus. The term can also be used to measure the even or uneven spread of a word or phrase through a text or texts (e.g., terms appearing frequently at the beginning of a text but nowhere else are not evenly spread; whereas, terms appearing consistently in the beginning, middle, and end of the text are more evenly spread).

Distant Reading: an analysis method that identifies patterns describing the shape of data without examining individual data points. Examples may include word clouds, word frequency counts, and automated data coding.

Diversity: a characteristic of corpus design and creation, referring to the intentional representation of the full variety of language content (including speakers, contexts, purposes, registers, etc.) that a corpus is meant to represent.

Frequency: a) the number of times a word or phrase appears in a corpus, which may be represented as absolute (i.e., raw count) or relative (i.e., proportion of a whole) value; b) a tool built into corpus analysis software that is capable of counting occurrences of words or phrases.

Keyness: a measure of a word's importance to the meaning of a corpus or a text within that corpus. This importance may be expressed in a variety of statistical ways, including log-likelihood and log ratio. Each expression attempts to indicate whether a word's frequency is larger or smaller than what would be expected by comparison to a separate corpus used as a reference. Cf. *Positive Keyness* and *Negative Keyness*.

KWIC: a) an acronym standing for Key Word In Context, meaning a word or phrase plus its immediate textual context; b) a tool built into corpus analysis software that is capable of locating words or phrases and presenting them with words to the left or right that constitute the immediate context. Cf. *Concordance*.

Lemma: the base form of a word from which other forms may be derived to serve other grammatical and syntactic functions in discourse. For example: written, writer, writers, and writerly derive from the lemma *write*. Lemmas are often presented with an asterisk after the letters forming the lemma to indicate "all words beginning with these letters and closing with any ending" (e.g., searching for the lemma *write** would return write, writes, writer, writers, and writerly).

Lemmatization: a) the process of choosing and creating lemmas; b) the process of analyzing a collection of words derived from a single lemma.

Lexicography: an area of study within corpus linguistics referring to the analysis of word meaning, usage, and change. Lexicographic analysis may involve tracking word usage to identify changes in meaning and use over the course of time, in different contexts of use, or among different people.

N-gram: a) a unit of language describing a grouping of immediately adjacent words where "N" refers to the number of words comprising the unit (e.g., 3–gram = three-word phrase); b) a tool built into corpus analysis software that is capable of locating and listing sequential groupings of words with a specified "N" length value.

Negative Keyness: a measure of a word's lack of importance to the meaning of a corpus or a text within that corpus. This lack of importance may be expressed in a variety of statistical ways, including log-likelihood and log ratio. Each expression attempts to indicate whether a word's frequency is smaller than what would be expected by comparison to a corpus used as a reference. Cf. *Keyness* and *Positive Keyness*.

Population: the full universe of texts comprising the discourse that a corpus represents in part. For example: a corpus of software user documentation comes from a population of all software user documentation.

Positive Keyness: a measure of word's importance to the meaning of a corpus or a text within that corpus. This importance may be expressed in a variety of statistical ways, including log-likelihood and log ratio. Each expression attempts to indicate whether a word's frequency is larger than what would be expected by comparison to a corpus used as a reference. Cf. *Keyness* and *Negative Keyness*.

Proportional Representation: expresses a word's frequency in a corpus as a percentage of the whole set of words (or phrases) in the corpus. The figure may also be represented as a normalized value projected per 10,000 words. Also called "relative frequency."

Register: Uses of language that are specific to a distinctive situation. Related to the concept of genre, but more constrained to the presence or absence of recurrent words or phrases.

Relative Frequency: Cf. *proportional representation.*

Representativeness: "the extent to which a sample includes the full range of variability in a population" (Biber, 1993, p. 243).

Saturation: a point during the analysis process when a researcher stops finding examples that expand the theoretical criteria that are germane to the study. In other words, saturation is when a researcher has found all the categories or findings that are relevant to the study at hand.

Study Corpus: In comparative studies: the corpus that is under investigation. Sometimes called "target corpus." Cf. *Reference Corpus.*

Reference Corpus: In comparative studies: the corpus being used to create contrast with the study corpus. Cf. *study corpus.*

Thin Description: The process of describing a phenomena based on a limited reading of a large number of data points. The process is the opposite of thick description, which describes a phenomena based on a detailed reading of a limited number of data points. Cf. *Distant Reading.*